FULFILLING OUR BEST POSSIBILITES
AS INDIVIDUALS AND AS A SOCIETY

NAVIGATING THE MAZEWAY

ANTHONY J. PARROTTO

WHITMORE PUBLISHING CO.
PITTSBURGH, PA 15222

ISBN: 978-0-87426-072-4

Printed in the United States of America

First Printing

For more information or to order additional books, please contact:
Whitmore Publishing Co.
926 Liberty Avenue
Pittsburgh, PA 15222
U.S.A.
1-866-451-1966
www.whitmorebooks.com

Dedicated to those
with the courage and the will
to seek their true identity
and actualize their best possibilities.

CONTENTS

I

THROUGH THE LOOKING GLASS

Out yonder is this huge world which exists
independently of human beings and
which stands before us like a great eternal riddle,
at least partially accessible to our inspection
and thinking. Nature has a character of
such a well-designed puzzle.

- ALBERT EINSTEIN

THE LOOKING GLASS

When I was a youngster, I assumed there were many wise and imaginative leaders who were managing our institutions to ensure a viable future. I believed the school principal, our pastor, congressmen, the mayor, the president, and other leaders always knew what they were doing and always had our best interests in mind. The discovery that this perception was largely an illusion has disturbed me ever since. I changed from an ordinary young person struggling to adapt to the world as it was into someone compelled to learn how the world worked, or ought to work, and how I might consciously model my life based on my own sensibilities, rather than leaving it to others to prescribe.

In the story that follows, I explain what brought me to "the looking glass" to examine our institutions and myself. I could have easily submitted to conventional wisdom by doing what was expected of me. However, when I began to generate challenging questions that my intuition supported and others could not successfully dismiss, I knew I was passing through the looking glass to the other side, where the perspective was much broader. From there, I was driven to continue my exploration. I was unaware it was the beginning point of a lifelong mission that would propel me, through agony and ecstasy, beyond my limitations.

Throughout the years of my search for the truth, I did not feel shame when I asked dumb questions, as long as I uttered them with humility. I may have been naïve and did not know what I did not know, but at least I would try to pursue knowledge without my ego driving the process and without illusion being its cornerstone. Occasionally, I would be called "too idealistic." I eventually found this amusing. I began perceiving others, who were content with the status quo, as being lazy, fearful, or simply unable to imagine a better alternative. It wasn't that I needed them to agree with me. Instead, I wished they would enter the debate, think more critically and holistically, and strive to realize what is possible and noble for us and for our society.

At the time I did not recognize that being able to see the social process from both sides of the looking glass would give me an advantage in my personal life, in business, and in what was to become a transcendent journey through "the mazeway."

THE MAZEWAY

I define the mazeway as:

- you, me, and everyone else
- functioning within the social process of this planet
- situated in the riddle of the universe

A puzzle within a puzzle within a puzzle.

No maps or instruction manuals come with the puzzles. Instead, we are surrounded by many institutions and individuals who offer their perspective about how the world works or ought to work, and how we should model our lives. We hardly realize we function as both props and players within the drama of the mazeway. We are props to the degree we remain passive and unaware. We are players to the degree we pursue our life's journey consciously and creatively in order to discover and to fulfill our best possibilities as unique individuals. These observations prompt challenging questions:

- How do we develop a clear vision of who we are?
- What should we value, believe, and think?
- How do we then actualize our best possibilities as individuals and as a society?

I believe very few of us are prepared to answer such questions adequately. Through social conditioning and a highly fragmented educational process, through fear and a lack of curiosity, and through the institutionalization of power and control, most of us are imprisoned conceptually within a twilight zone of awareness in which we delude ourselves that we are oriented and free in the mazeway.

We *do* enjoy the benefits of democracy and a market economy, but few of us are aware that we are not free in the fullest sense. We do not realize how much our identity and behavior are shaped for us by others, and how much we are held captive by the imperatives of the mythos of our times.

Shaping us are overarching institutions such as religion, government, and educational curricula, as well as other powerful constructs such as political and marketing campaigns. There is also a pervasive wild card now at play in the human drama: the mass media. Together, these various social constructs shape what we think and how we behave much more than we realize.

We are consumers of beliefs down to details concerning what clothes we should wear, what foods we should eat, and what constitutes an enviable lifestyle and an attractive or sexy body. We are also purveyors of beliefs to the extent that we disseminate our own point of view to our progeny and to others. As consumers of beliefs, we can be either beneficiaries or victims: some maps help illuminate the way, while others contain misdirection that undermines our potential, and may lead to disaster.

Herein lies the crucible of the human drama—the ongoing struggle to differentiate between perceptions of right and wrong, between what leads to light and to darkness, between how the world works and how it ought to work. This drama plays itself out within each of us and through the dynamics of the social process.

In my own case, I struggled to become oriented and truly free in the mazeway, wanting to be in control of my existence based on my *own* thoughts, feelings, and deep inner self. I questioned the arbitrariness of the prescriptions proposed by others. Which were valid? Which were false? I wondered whether there was one square foot of truth on which to build a coherent view of reality and a credible life. Strangely, my journey toward clarity began with a health problem.

THE TWILIGHT ZONE OF HEALTH

By age 27 my life's journey seemed to be more circuitous than that of most young men struggling to adapt to the world as it was in 1958. A five-year degree program in Business Administration at Drexel University was punctuated by three years in the military during the Korean War, which included Marine boot camp, eight months at sea on an aircraft carrier as a corporal, and then 13 months as a cadet in Naval Flight School. Along the way I experienced several love affairs, as well as a series of jobs I had trouble taking seriously. Through all the zigging and zagging that characterized my life at that time, I was tormented by an elusive health problem that traditional medical practice was not able to solve. I will spare you the details except to say that I needed to retreat to my own sensibilities to deal with my dilemma. I could not depend on established protocols. This was part of the mazeway that I would need to learn to navigate on my own.

Over time I discovered I suffered from food sensitivities and allergies, which 47 years ago were still a mystery to most medical doctors.

From this experience I concluded that: I was not in full health; nor was I in a state of disease. I was in what I began to call the Twilight Zone of Health, a subtle state between the two.

I speculated that there must be many millions of people who are neither sick nor in full health, but were suffering from symptoms of one kind or another that were sub-clinical. And, while physicians can certainly be heroes to us, they and their set of techniques were not particularly good at dealing with those who find themselves in the Twilight Zone of Health.

What struck me clearly was the imperfection and imbalance of the doctor/patient relationship. The absolute power granted to the physician undermined the patient in the process. The concept of a full exchange of information was an illusion. The actual approach was a shortsighted, top-down management of the patient.

These observations helped me generate the concept of Body Wisdom long before the book on the subject was published. (See the reference stated below.) I use the term to mean that we, as individuals, normally know more about many of the subtleties and peculiarities of our own bodies than physicians or instruments can discern. The more knowledge we accrue about how to manage our bodies and maintain full health, the better—and the greater likelihood of realizing our life expectancy.

When we do interact with a physician, we need to empower ourselves. We must participate rather than submit. We need to remember that we are the clients, and medical doctors are the service providers working for us. Their special status has been granted by our respect for their knowledge and skills. However, we must be prepared to question their assumptions and conclusions, since they can err.

Today, appreciation for Body Wisdom and other such insights are much more commonplace. In 1996 Dr. Ann Tyndall published *Body Wisdom—The Longevity of Lifestyle*.[52] And there are others such as *Anatomy of the Spirit* by Dr. Caroline Myss.[37] You can now hear in our everyday language references to preventive medicine and how our lifestyles relate to our health. An alternative medicine industry has been flourishing and fills the gaps that the science-based medical model does not satisfy. However, 47 years ago those who thought in such a way were marginalized. If it did not fit the current paradigm, if it were not science-based, or if it did not come down from the theocracy of the profession, the notion was deemed questionable at best, probably wrong, and dismissed.

I was learning that common sense can easily be abandoned for the sake of honoring protocols that are advanced by established institutions, whether they are medical, religious, educational, economic, or political. Despite the fact that protocols change over time, many practitioners honor current ones so absolutely that they close their minds to new possibilities. Such myopia can lead to misfortune.

When we apply this insight to us as individuals, we do not perceive ourselves as naïve and confined within one set of assumptions or another on the traditional side of the looking glass. This is understandable since almost everyone around us is also naïve and confined.

TO THE OTHER SIDE

Some of us, as a result of a traumatic, eye-opening experience, find ourselves questioning conventional wisdom, since what we have encountered cannot be explained adequately through it. For me, it was my health problem that pressed me to challenge the assumptions of the established medical model. Actually, my moment of profound illumination occurred during my research into the concept of Body Wisdom. It was when I stumbled upon Abraham H. Maslow's "hierarchy of needs model."[34]

Professor Maslow, who was chairman of the Department of Psychology at Brandeis University, recognized that beyond our physical needs, we have psychological needs such as safety, recognition, belongingness, love, and self-esteem. At the top of this hierarchy is the need to transcend what appear to be our limitations and actualize our best possibilities.

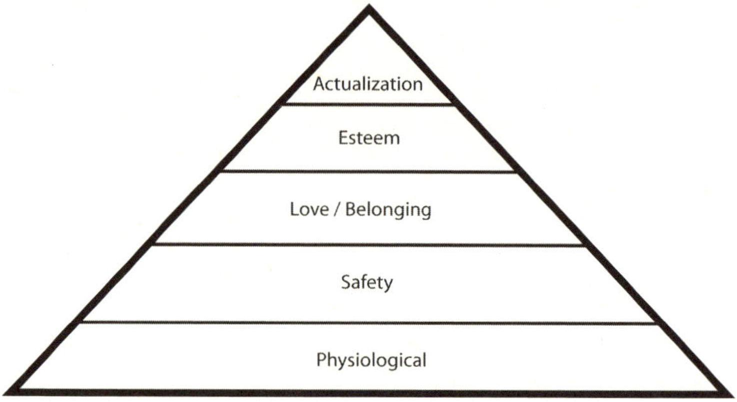

HIERARCHY OF HUMAN NEEDS

While his model impressed me, I would probably have skipped by it as just another interesting insight about the human condition. However, because I had been questioning the medical model and trying to develop the concept of Body Wisdom, I was struck by how well the hierarchy of needs model provided a meaningful framework for understanding what drives us forward during our life's journey. I could understand that my quest to gain Body Wisdom was simply one step along the way toward self-actualization.

As I pondered the significance of Maslow's elegant model along with my other thoughts and feelings, I became very upset. To my surprise, I rose from my chair and, uncharacteristically, slammed Maslow's book down on my desk and exclaimed to myself that "the system had failed me." I discerned in that moment of anger that the objective of education and our other institutions should be to help us become whole and free and empowered as individuals, rather than make it seem natural to become fragmented, submissive cogs in an incomprehensible wheel of the socio-economic machine of our time. Maslow's model enabled me to conceptualize the crucial variable that is missing from the equation of the educational process—a variable that would help make the highly fragmented, traditional curriculum much more coherent and empowering.

This moment of truth drove me to question the premises of all major institutions to see where it would lead me. A long, circuitous inquiry ensued during which the following questions presented themselves:

- Should not the nurturing of the individual and his or her wholeness and freedom be the primary objective of our institutions?
- Wouldn't more independent-minded and comprehensively aware citizens help sustain a free society better than those who are highly fragmented and trained primarily to follow?
- If, in the past, leaders in education felt compelled to develop a subdivided curriculum based on industrial-age

modeling, did they realize the long-term consequences? Did they throw away the key to how students could recompose the fragments of knowledge in a coherent manner?

- Don't we eventually run a risk of lacking the leadership required to manage increasingly complex organizations if each succeeding generation increases the emphasis on specialization?
- If we pull back the curtain behind which our leaders shield themselves, will we find most of them naked in terms of their ability to envision and shape a viable future?
- Would there be fewer casualties of the system, e.g., disorientation, alienation, addiction, stress, mental breakdown, disease, and poverty, if we were taught an unvarnished and more holistic vision of the mazeway?

These are the kinds of strategic questions I wished to have answered. I was less interested in tactical inquiries and efforts to "patch" what's wrong with this or that *part* of a program. Typically, patching leads nowhere because it does not rework basic premises.

And so it was Maslow's exquisite model that led me to the looking glass to examine myself and our institutions—such a long time ago. The encounter turned out to be a pivotal event in my life. As I mentioned earlier, I would have simply passed by Maslow's thesis had I not been in the process of challenging the medical model and trying to flesh out the concept of Body Wisdom. His insights were intellectual and emotional catalysts for me. They amplified my view of the world, and reminded me of my need to question authority, to avoid being controlled by others, to honor my intuition, and to shape my life consciously.

I could *now* discern more clearly the natural progression of my inquiry which I began on the subject of health. The concept of Body Wisdom prompted me to explore the possibilities of accruing Emotional Wisdom and, ultimately, Spiritual Wisdom—three inextricably related dimensions of awareness we need to actualize, if we are to fulfill our best possibilities.

I was surprised when questions that Maslow's insights prompted me to ask were not readily satisfied by others. Instead, I was getting half-baked answers which seemed to confirm that my perceptions were valid. Once I began suspecting conventional wisdom was questionable, if not riddled with illusions, I found myself passing through the looking glass to the other side where the perspective was much broader. As if a switch were turned on, I realized that the simple act of challenging the assumptions of established institutions propelled me to conceptual freedom on the other side. From that moment on I was no longer a part of the malleable masses, unaware of the arbitrariness of assumptions of our institutions. I was free to discover how the pieces of the puzzles of our existence fit together from my own point of view.

I quickly recognized the advantage of being able to view both sides of the looking glass. And like Lewis Carroll's Alice, the world I found on the other side reflected back on the world I'd just emerged from. From this new vantage point, I could view conventional wisdom, and, at the same time, explore dimensions outside its containment.

From that time on, I was to be the quiet revolutionary, discontented with the status quo, asking questions, and scheming to generate an action plan that would enable me and others to become whole and free and empowered.

No, I had not lost my mind. I knew I could function in the conventional world and adapt to its demands. I also knew that I need not accept that manner of living without reservation. I could function on both sides of the looking glass and see where my expanding conception of the mazeway would lead me.

THREE GOALS

As my life unfolded, three overarching goals drove me forward, as I confronted challenging questions about myself and the world around me:

1. Climb the highest mountain I could to gain a universal worldview. That is, try to resolve an inclusive perspective free of contradictions whose premises would be valid forever. I would not seek this, if I thought any of our institutions were providing it.
2. Based on what I learned pursuing my first goal, design an educational strategy that would empower us, individually and collectively, to become whole and free to fulfill our best possibilities. I call this initiative The Mazeway Project.
3. Become financially independent so that I would be free to pursue my other goals without material constraints affecting the outcome.

Of course I realized that this combination of goals would test my limitations and raise questions about my sanity. My strategy was to trust my inherent sensibilities and trek forward carefully without being seduced by dead-end mental models and/or deleterious lifestyles. Otherwise, there was no way of knowing if I possessed the perseverance and wherewithal to meet these challenges.

II

TOWARD A UNIVERSAL PERSPECTIVE

Nothing has meaning except in terms of its context,
its connection with something larger,
so that the process of discovering truth
is the process of extending one's knowledge.

- LOUIS J. HALLE. *Out of Chaos* [23]

DELUSIONS PREVAIL

Being serious about seeking a universal perspective seems strange to most people. Why would anyone waste his time and energy on such a nebulous, if not impossible, search? It is hoped I will be able to explain the reason, now that I have gained a glimpse of how the pieces of the puzzle fit together.

I will begin by expressing my amazement at the mindlessness and unending chaos humans generate. On and on, over the centuries, we have suffered from war, hunger, poverty, and other dispiriting misfortunes. It doesn't seem to matter how sophisticated and resourceful we become; we have *not* been able to break the cycle of misadventures, destruction, and despair. Unfortunately, delusions prevail over any wisdom we accrue, as we brazenly impose our will and our certainty on each other. What are the sources of our delusions and arrogance? What is the origin of our prejudices and self-limiting ideologies that generate so much pain, suffering, and underachievement? From my point of view, there is something fundamentally erroneous being perpetuated and I have been intent on discovering what it is.

I searched the mazeway over a period of many years. While I learned all kinds of interesting things, it was not until I stumbled on the phenomenon of "programs of the mind" that I began to understand the basis of our predicament.

PROGRAMS OF THE MIND

As you will recall, I defined the mazeway as you, me, and everyone else, functioning within the social process of this planet, situated in the riddle of the universe—a puzzle within a puzzle within a puzzle. The drama of humankind is really the story of our efforts over the millennia to comprehend and navigate the mazeway in order to satisfy our physical, psychological, and spiritual needs. To cope with these challenges, we have had to rely on three components of our being: hardware, firmware, and software.

Hardware and Firmware

The hardware component of our being comprises the physical substance of our body: its cells, tissues, organs, and systems.

The firmware includes our particular genetic makeup, which largely determines (a) our physical attributes, (b) our intelligence, and (c) our temperament and a range of innate capabilities.

The hardware and firmware components of our being establish the fundamental basis from which we proceed through life. While we cannot easily change these factors, we can test their limits and maximize our potential. Whether or not we realize our potential depends, to a large extent, on the third component of our being—the software.

Software

The software component constitutes the programs of the mind or thought patterns we acquire through exposure to our culture. Religion, government, schools, and the family are the institutions primarily responsible for "installing" programs of the mind. These include traditions, ideologies, and theories, along with their accompanying premises, values, and beliefs. The programs of the mind are social constructs promulgated by our institutions for understanding how the mazeway works and how we fit into it.

Our family and its particular situation are most important because the combination determines our religious upbringing, the schools we attend, and the environment within which we develop. The encoding process occurs primarily during our formative years, ostensibly with the best of intentions. As natural as taking on the language of one's family, the programs of the mind are assimilated bit by bit. Imperceptibly, they become an integral part of our being. We are not in a position during our early years to challenge them very much, nor do we have much of a sense of the inculcation process. There is little conscious understanding that the outcome could have been dramatically different had we been raised within another family system in some other part of the world. As we mature, the programs become fixed, more or less. We are not encouraged to question them. Instead, most of the programs prompt us to seek out affirmation of what we already value and believe, i.e., what has been prescribed and proscribed.

Assimilated in this manner, the programs of the mind determine the religion we may practice, our view of politics, economics, the family, and our individual self, as well as our perceptions of society and the world in general. The sum of these constitutes our worldview.

Our worldview (frame of reference, philosophy of life, belief system) prescribes the limits and bounds of our life's journey and how we will interpret our experience. The narrower our perspective, the more limited our range of possibilities. The broader our perspective, the greater our capacity to comprehend and navigate the mazeway.

Therefore, on one hand, we have "nature"—the hardware and firmware components of our being governed by our genetic makeup. On the other hand, we have "nurture"—the software components of our being, i.e., programs of the mind, which we acquire through exposure to our culture—an arbitrary affair based less on conscious choice than on the accident of the time and place of birth and our family's orientation.

It was at this point that I began to understand the basis of our wisdom, as well as the basis of our foolishness. To a great extent, our behavior is shaped by the set of arbitrary, intuitively formulated programs inculcated in us during the nurturing process. And, since it is very difficult to step outside the influence of these mental models, we are not in a position to judge them objectively. Our egocentricity, provincialism, and certainty lock us into a particular orientation. Consequently, we remain unaware that the programs encoded in us can *either* enhance our development *or* undermine it—they can *either* liberate us *or* imprison us.

In these terms, we have two identities. One is imposed by the culture around us; the other comprises our true self—the essence of our uniqueness at the core of our being which would express itself if we were free and empowered. I suspect that most of us are conceptually imprisoned and will never realize our true identity. This is because the programs of the mind advanced by our institutions are so commanding that it is very difficult for us to transcend them. As a result, we are more likely to seek only affirmation rather than question the programs that are the basis of our worldview.

I believe, if we are to avoid following conventional wisdom blindly, and if we are to gain our true identity, we must learn how programs of the mind are created in the first place. What follows is an intuitive, highly generalized perception of how they are generated.

LANGUAGE

Imagine early humans struggling to survive their predicament. As they uttered the first semblance of a word—that earliest conscious grunt—they were simply trying to use whatever mental attributes they had inherent in them to meet the challenge of the moment. Somehow one such utterance became accepted as meaning something specific to the group. Whenever the word was spoken, everyone knew what it meant. Over what was probably a very long period of time, new words and symbols were added until the language of the group evolved into an organized system of communication. That invention turned out to be a pivotal event in the evolution of humans.

Language enabled members of the group to convey thoughts and feelings among themselves. And then it empowered them to use their system of words and symbols as building blocks to create social instruments: how they would interact with each other and with their environment; how to secure food, water, and shelter; and how to satisfy their psychological needs, including how to allay their fears and explain the many mysteries surrounding them. Language not only provided the means to describe the world, it provided the tool for "creating" it. Language also made it possible to pass on to future generations what they had learned and created in the form of stories. *The stories and the myths that emerged became the programs of the mind that established the bases for their institutions and the shape of their culture.*

The systems of words and symbols that early humans employed defined their reality, including their individual and collective identity. Without language there would be no identity; there would be no institutions; there would be no culture.

Today we are surrounded by innumerable religious, political, and economic ideologies, as well as scientific theories that form the programs of the mind and worldviews that frame our existence. Without the development of language, none of this would have been possible.

WORLDVIEWS

It was illuminating for me to learn about the following differentiation of worldviews.

Premodern Worldview

Premodern worldviews were based *either* on revelation *or* on human inquiry.

A "revealed" worldview constituted a perception of reality that emerged gradually, took hold and, typically, became a fixed belief system *perceived to be engendered by a god* and sustained by tradition. Examples of revealed worldviews are Judaism, Christianity, and Islam.

On the other hand, a "non-revealed" worldview constituted a perception of reality that also emerged gradually, took hold, and was sustained by tradition. But, instead of being ordained by a god, *it was generated through human inquiry*, that is, through the thoughts, feelings, and imagination of individuals. Examples of non-revealed worldviews include Buddhism and Taoism.

In the distant past there was little perspective about the worldviews others embraced, since there was minimal travel and exposure to other perspectives. The possibility that there might be other groups with substantially different belief systems was either not imagined or such thoughts were repressed. Those in charge believed it was their responsibility to perpetuate the established worldview, while everyone else was compelled to follow along. There was not much questioning of *the possibility* that elements of the established belief system could be at odds with objective reality, or that those worldviews, which are considered to be revealed, were simply *intuitional creations* that satisfied hopes and fears, rather than being engendered by a god as irrevocable declarations. Premodern worldviews prevail to this day after thousands of years.

Modern Worldview

The modern worldview emerged when travel increased and exposure to other cultures took place. An ever-increasing number of people recognized there were realities different from their own. This insight prompted some individuals and groups to propose new ideas that were at odds with the established order of things. These challenges led to hostile reactions, resulting in inquisitions, revolutions, and other forms of holy wars, as each group battled to defend what it believed to be the real truth. Some people place the roots of the modern worldview as far back as the time of Socrates and Plato. Others perceive it was shepherded in by the Enlightenment and the Scientific Method.

The clash between premodern and modern worldviews continues to this day. It is a struggle *between* belief systems. That struggle is now being exacerbated by the postmodern worldview, which generates contention concerning beliefs *about* beliefs.[1]

Postmodern Worldview

High-speed travel and global communications brought us into a world where we are constantly exposed to a wide range of values, beliefs, and opinions. We see religions competing with one another and different sociopolitical ideologies struggling for dominance. What has emerged from this fertile milieu is the perception of sociologists, psychologists, and others that programs of the mind are social constructions of reality. This means that all ideas about human reality are social inventions created by human beings—that what is "real" and what is "not real" is not determined by an external deity, but by the way we see, name, and classify our experience through language. Therefore, since the programs of the mind were conceived and developed by humans, we are free to modify or reinvent them for our time. Instead of *absolute* values ordained by a deity *or* generated through human inquiry, there are only *relative* values based on the context of the situation. This conception, born in the twentieth century, has been characterized as the postmodern worldview.[1]

Modern-day intellectuals discuss ever more frequently the challenge postmodernists have imposed. Many express deep concern about the turmoil that may result from the deconstruction of the basic premises of established belief systems. Aware that this presents a dilemma to humankind of incalculable importance, many philosophers, theologians, and other scholars press their limits to conceive a context within which to place all that has come forward, and to wonder what should constitute a more inclusive vision of our reality that would lead us forward creatively as individuals, as societies, and as a species.

Integral Worldview

I think it is clear that postmodernism is *not* the endpoint of the unfolding of worldviews. It represents a transition to a broader and more integrated vision of the mazeway. Accordingly, I find myself identifying with those who are struggling to define an integral worldview—a perspective that honors the truths of each outlook that has come before, while proceeding forward as coherently as possible.

Seeing the concept of programs of the mind within the context of this delineation of worldviews became an important part of my evolving perspective. I felt a sense of further liberation and an empowerment to view the social process from the other side of the looking glass with greater clarity. *When I reached this point in my understanding, I realized that an integral worldview and the universal perspective I sought as a young man were the same.* I also realized that this adventure of mine was not simply a high-minded, quixotic quest to discover indisputable truths on which to build a credible life for myself. This is also a quest being pursued by an increasing number of other people who understand the profound limitations of worldviews described above as premodern, modern, and postmodern.

Stuck on the conventional side of the looking glass within provincial, self-limiting worldviews, most human beings do not realize that humankind is probably heading toward a disastrous future. Their egocentricity obscures the reality of the situation, as they conclude there must be something wrong with the point of view of others that is causing the growing number of problems. Their conceptual imprisonment makes it difficult if not impossible for them to realize how fragmentation, dualisms, alienation, polarization, and inflexible ideologies obscure their vision, while causing all kinds of misadventures, destruction, and despair. Anyone still awake and thinking realizes that this is not a prediction of what will happen some day. It is already happening, and you can bet it will get much worse if we ignore our predicament. We need a shift in consciousness to an increasingly integrated perspective—a perspective that will lead to a coherent and moral vision of how we can move forward together creatively, joyfully, and peacefully. What follows represents my own effort to gain such a perspective.

I continue this adventure of mind and spirit by exploring the pivotal point of my search, Page Zero.

PAGE ZERO

I first heard the term Page Zero many years ago when a business associate and I were learning how to use a new computer system being installed at my company. Toward the end of two days of training, the instructor explained, almost in a whisper, that we needed to learn about the variable parameters on Page Zero.

The instructor went on to explain that there were fundamental attributes to the computer program *that only those in charge should know about or change.* If this or that parameter of the program were changed, it would affect how the rest of the system worked. My employees, who would be using the application programs on a day-to-day basis, should not have access to the operating system's Page Zero and mess with the variables if we wanted to avoid chaos.

How interesting, I thought at the time. Intuitively I knew it was an important insight that related to social programs promoted by our institutions to control our behavior. I had no idea where and how the insight could be applied—until now.

I use the term Page Zero here to refer to the premises that underpin programs of the mind. *At the core of each program, on its Page Zero, is a set of premises which empowers the program.* When we follow a particular program, i.e., belief system, political ideology, etc., we do not need to know about or fully understand its premises to become a believer. Hardly any of us explore and/or challenge a program's fundamental rationale. We have been taught to be faithful and stay within bounds, as if inoculated against other points of view.

I think it is important to recognize that, if we do not clearly know the premises of the programs we subscribe to, we more or less follow the programs blindly. To the degree they are valid, we become beneficiaries. But if they are defective, we become victims. As I mentioned earlier, some programs help illuminate the way, while others contain coding that undermines our potential, if not our survival.

In these terms, the more coherent and relevant the premises on Page Zero, the more likely the programs and the institutions that embody them will remain viable and continue to evolve. Examples include democratic government and a market economy—at least in their purest form.

On the other hand, history is replete with programs of the mind and institutions that failed because their premises were fundamentally flawed and/or became irrelevant for the times. Recent examples include Soviet Communism, Fascism, and Nazism, the disastrous results of which are clear in our minds.

Accordingly, it seems sensible to me to learn about the premises on the Page Zeros of the programs that drive our institutions, as well as the premises on Page Zeros of the programs that shape our individual lives. What is the basis of those premises and how do we judge their validity within the context of our times, if not all times? Not to engage these questions diminishes our possibilities as individuals, as a culture, and as a species.

SEEING

I wondered whether it was really possible to gain an integral worldview. It's one thing to theorize and be wishful about such a notion; it's another to actually achieve it. Was it a matter of something we needed to learn or experience or create? In a recurring fantasy:

> I imagined those of us on the other side of the looking glass struggling within ourselves and debating with others as to where our blurry visions would guide us. We are compelled to discover new pathways that will lead us higher on the mountain. We venture onto cold, slippery slopes, taking risks. Encumbered by vestiges of beliefs we left behind, we fear, among other things, that we may

become caught in the looking glass itself, neither fully on one side nor the other. Should we retreat or go forward? It was so comfortable and secure within our prior orientation. Why did we ever abandon it?

We resolve that there is no turning back. We zigzag along, considering one point of view after another. We find interesting speculations but no coherent map for the rest of our journey.

We share our fears, our hopes, and our dreams. We sense that each of us possesses a part of the answer to our puzzle. What is the correct combination?

We agree to share our remaining provisions and to sacrifice whatever else may be required to enable as many of us as possible to continue. A bond of friendship heightens our spirit.

Each move forward becomes an act of courage and determination. Confusion and doubt haunt us, as the trails become increasingly obscure and treacherous. The air is thin and no safe retreat is in sight. The horizon that guides us now must be generated by our intuition, a subtle orchestration of the mind and heart, a test of our authenticity. It seems that each of us must travel the last leg of the journey alone.

Can we make it to the top? What will we see? What will we learn? What will we feel?

While you and I may not ever be able to answer these questions fully, I imagine those individuals who have or could answer them include such extraordinary people as: Socrates, Jesus, Mohammed, The Buddha, and Albert Einstein. It's as though they reached the top of the mountain and were able to perceive an endless horizon and beyond in a seamless, integral manner, and feel an inherent part of it all, if only fleetingly. We lack the language to describe their visions very well. (At least I am not able to describe it any better than I have.) I suspect that many more individuals have had such godlike attributes that enabled them to gain an integral vision of how the pieces of the puzzles of the mazeway fit together. The problem is that, up to now, humankind, as a whole, has failed to fulfill the promise of such leaps forward of mind and spirit. We have failed to build institutions that are vibrant and sustainable in a fashion that enables those who follow to continue their developmental journey and fulfill their own best possibilities. Somehow, given enough time, we end up with institutions that are, more often than not, egocentric, provincial, highly bureaucratized, corruptible, and otherwise self-limiting.

I believe we can do much better.

CONNECTING THE DOTS

I have touched upon a wide range of topics in this chapter. Before moving forward, I will summarize them here and try to connect the salient points.

- I began by asking: What are the sources of our delusions and arrogance? What is the origin of our prejudices and self-limiting ideologies that generate so much pain, suffering, and underachievement? These questions challenged me to understand and connect the phenomena of language, programs of the mind, worldviews, and Page Zero.
- Language has played a pivotal role in humankind's developmental journey. It empowered early humans to use their system of words and symbols as building blocks to create social instruments that would help them satisfy their physical, psychological, and spiritual needs. The stories and the myths that emerged became the programs of the mind that established the premises for their institutions and the shape of their culture.
- Religion, government, schools, and the family are the institutions primarily responsible for "installing" programs of the mind. The programs determine the religion we may practice, our view of politics, economics, the

family, and our individual self, as well as our perceptions of society and the world in general. The sum of these constitutes our worldview.

- The worldviews of humankind progressed over the centuries from premodern, to modern, to postmodern. Today, many of us realize that postmodernism is *not* the endpoint of the unfolding of worldviews. It represents a transition to gaining an integral perspective—an inclusive and coherent vision of the mazeway and our role within it.
- However, up to now, we have failed to fulfill the promise of the visions of prophets, shamans, and mystics, as well as the promise of what we have learned and what we have experienced otherwise. We find ourselves stuck within provincial and otherwise self-limiting ideologies of premodern, modern, and postmodern worldviews—worldviews that have led, and continue to lead humankind, to an endless cycle of misadventures, destruction, and despair.
- Clearly, we need a shift in consciousness to an increasingly integral perspective. I believe this shift will occur when we more fully understand that it is the coding we do on Page Zero that largely determines the outcomes of the human drama. It is there that we formulate the premises that become the bases of the programs of the mind that frame our existence. Will we continue to follow a provincial, self-limiting worldview, or will we strive to gain an integral worldview that will lead to a coherent and moral vision of how we can move forward together creatively, joyfully, and peacefully?

MATERIALISTIC OR TRANSPERSONAL LENS?

The summary above leads us to another challenging question: Will we grasp an integral perspective by viewing our reality through a "materialist lens" or a "transpersonal lens," or through some combination of the two?

To differentiate these lenses, I insert here a quote from the Foreword that John E. Mack, M.D. wrote for the book, *Paths Beyond Ego*.[53]

"We are witnessing a battle for the human soul between two opposing ontologies (theories of existence). In one view, the physical or material world is the ultimate, if not the only, reality, and the behaviors and experiences of living organisms, including ourselves, can be understood within the framework of potentially identifiable mechanisms. In this worldview consciousness is a function of the human brain, and its furthest reaches and greatest depths are, in theory, fathomable through the researches of neuroscience and psychodynamic formulations. In this view, life is a finite game.

"In the transpersonal view, the physical world and all its laws represent only one of an indeterminable number of possible realities whose qualities we can only begin to apprehend through the evolution of our consciousness. In this view, consciousness pervades all realities and is the primary source or creative principle of existence, including the energy-matter of the physical world. Until recently, Western philosophy and science, including psychology, have been dominated by the first view. The transpersonal vision is opening our minds, hearts, and spirits to the second. In this view, life is an infinite game."

I believe, if we are to gain an integral worldview, we must combine the attributes of both lenses. But how do we reconcile a reliance on gaining truth through the senses with a reliance on gaining truth through faith? How do we reconcile the focus on changing the external world through science, technology, and relative values with a focus on changing the internal world through absolute values and the pursuit of transcendental wisdom? How do we reconcile a view of life as a finite game with a view of life as an infinite game, within which the only truth is in the spirit of the eternal?

It seems foolish to me to make it be an either-or proposition, since both lenses illuminate our journey in the mazeway.

Various combinations are possible. Keep in mind that the mazeway itself has been functioning coherently and creatively long before humankind came along. It is we who struggle to orient ourselves in an inclusive and coherent manner, and to reconcile our differences. Because we did not have maps and instruction manuals (lenses) to guide us when we began our journey in the mazeway, we had to do the best we could to make sense of our reality. We needed to compose stories and myths that would become the programs of the mind that established the premises for our institutions and the shape of the various cultures that ensued.

Given the fact that countless enclaves of humans were separated from one another and were confronted by different circumstances, we should not be surprised that the stories and myths (lenses) humans developed through the ages would be different. However, given the fact that the lenses came from the *same* species, it seems obvious to me that they are reconcilable.

Unfortunately, up to now, we have been suffering from profound myopia. Instead of questioning our orientation and its premises, instead of seeking reconciliation and a more integral perspective, most of us simply seek affirmation of what we already believe. As I mentioned earlier, the world around us may be coming unhinged; yet, we conclude there must be something wrong with the point of view of others that is leading to problems. Most of us do not realize that, if we are to continue our developmental journey, individually and collectively, we must transcend our egocentricity and grasp a more inclusive and coherent vision of the mazeway.

MIND OF GOD

I believe the challenge of reconciliation and of synthesis is a test of our being—a test of our capacity to access the natural moral force within us. You may call this inherent capacity whatever you wish, such as "truth," "love," "infinite mind,"

"Holy Spirit," "absolute spirit," "soul," or "the mind of God." I settled on the phrase the mind of God, which I define as a gestalt of our mental faculties—the sum of our thoughts, feelings, intuition, imagination, and conscience. The combination of these attributes, functioning in an integrated, resonant manner, can propel us to a higher level of consciousness within which we transcend our egocentricity. In this special state, we experience a direct connection to the infinite-enfolded truth of quantum reality—clarity of knowing beyond knowledge—a sense of time before time—a glimpse of the whole, seamless vision of the mazeway. As an inherent part of the implicate order, the mind of God within us is the ultimate moral compass, our source of creativity, the means to our liberation and further development.

We access the mind of God when we are quiet and peaceful, and motivated by love and selflessness. This may occur through deep meditation, prayer, uplifting rituals, artful music, and other such experiences that help our mental faculties to resonate as one.

However, as mere humans, we may misread our moral compass, i.e., misunderstand the mind of God within us. We may believe that the visions it reveals came from a God separate from us, a God ruling the mazeway in a literal sense. As plausible as such perceptions might be, I think they lead to traps within the mazeway that have had, and continue to have, very serious consequences.

I believe we misunderstand the mind of God within us when we fail to honor its capacity to reason, its need for coherence. Reason is the variable within the equating action of the mind of God within us that will enable us to reconcile our differences and navigate the mazeway more fruitfully. On the other hand, absolute faith, however comforting it may be, separates us and may lead to holy wars and dead-ends in the mazeway.

RELIGION

As the history of humankind indicates, religion can *inhibit* our development, or it can *catalyze* it; it can be a *destructive* force, or a *creative* one

On one hand, once humans believe their visions came from a God separate from themselves, they are inclined to interpret the visions *literally.* As a result, the stories and myths that emerge from these literal interpretations *embody precepts that are believed to be irrefutable.* These absolutes are institutionalized into a rigid system of beliefs that frames the life of its followers. Closed and absolute, the system rejects new knowledge that may challenge established premises, and rejects reinterpretation of the original stories and myths. Consequently, the faithful are often imprisoned by stagnant precepts, superstition, prejudice, and illusion, along with fear of everlasting punishment based on strict rules of right and wrong invented eons ago under circumstances much different than we face today. Such orientations of certainty may comfort followers, but diminish curiosity and creativity. And, as the patterns of history suggest, they can lead to arrogance and tyrannical faith, which may justify all kinds of transgressions and atrocities executed in the name of God. It is not a matter that the visions and the interpretation of them are wrong, per se; it is more a matter that followers choose to preclude the possibilities of gaining a more inclusive and coherent perspective—an integral vision within which there may be no distinction between the mind of God within us and the mind of God beyond us.

On the other hand, our development is catalyzed when the religion provides principles of thought and modes of behavior that are open-ended and evolving—an orientation that encourages us to use our godlike attributes to be co-creators of our reality. Within such an empowering framework, we learn to trust our moral sensibility, which enables us to gain order and purpose in our lives, and to work constructively with others. The combination of these factors provides a catalyst for fulfilling our best possibilities, individually and collectively.

As I mentioned above, religion can *inhibit* our development, or it can *catalyze* it; it can be a *destructive* force, or a *creative* one. Therein lies the crucible of the human drama—the ongoing struggle to differentiate between perceptions of right and wrong, between what leads to light and to darkness, between what is true and what is false. This drama plays itself out within each of us and through the dynamics of the social process.

GOOD AND EVIL

I speculate that, just as there is order and chaos in the physical universe, there is good and evil, and, therefore, both divine and demonic attributes that lurk within our being, ready to manifest themselves as we make choices during our lifetime. Accordingly, the precepts we employ to frame our existence can be benevolent, coherent, and reflect the mind of God, or they can be at odds with the implicate order and contain malevolence and contradictions that reflect our dark side. As human beings, we have the potential to be either creative or destructive.

Therefore, if we are to generate light instead of darkness, if we are to experience serenity instead of anxiety, we need to combine honesty, humility, love, and compassion while subordinating our ego and seeking truth. Our whole being—our premises, values, beliefs, and opinions; how we think, feel, and behave—must be congruent with the implicate order of the mazeway which we need to perceive intuitively. In this moral state we reveal our divine attributes through our creative expressions, whether they be how we orchestrate our individual life, how we help design our institutions, or how we compose poetry, plays, music, and other works of art. When we are creating, we are using our highest faculties. In such process we are godlike.

We remain at lower levels of consciousness and generate darkness when we are dishonest, arrogant, jealous, egocentric, hateful, and/or exclusive. In this less moral state, our evil side reveals itself through the product of our total being. At odds with the implicate order, we directly or indirectly generate displeasing if not destructive effects, while the puzzles of the mazeway remain indecipherable. Therefore, how we choose to play our part in the drama of the mazeway determines how much light or darkness we bring to our own life and to the world around us.

MY SECOND GOAL

As I mentioned earlier, an integral worldview and the universal perspective I sought as a young man were the same. I also noted that this illusive goal is being pursued by an increasing number of other individuals who understand the profound limitations of premodern, modern, and postmodern worldviews.

Thus far, my effort to gain clarity has been very rewarding. Among other benefits, the process of assembling this *perspective about perspectives* has enabled me to flesh out the rationale and framework for an educational strategy that empowers us to become whole and free to fulfill our best possibilities, individually and collectively. As you will recall, I established this as my second goal, which I named The Mazeway Project.

III

THE MAZEWAY PROJECT

History becomes more and more
a race between education and disaster.

- H.G. WELLS

WELCOME TO THE MAZEWAY PROJECT

The premises of The Mazeway Project are reflected in the following suggestions:

- We, as individuals, are the basic unit of the social process, the authentic carrier of reality, not our institutions per se. If not enough of us get our own life together and dare to be great, we should not expect that our institutions will.
- We should take responsibility for our life based on our own thoughts, feelings and deep inner self, rather than leave it to others to prescribe.
- We should strive to become open-minded and universally oriented, rather than remain trapped within prejudices, illusions, and self-limiting ideologies.
- We should collaborate with others creatively to build self-catalyzing, self-cleansing, sustainable institutions that are responsive to the needs of all humankind.

The Mazeway Project appeals to those who are intellectually curious, emotionally resilient, and who possess the courage to question their assumptions and the assumptions of established institutions, not knowing where that will lead.

What follows establishes the rationale and framework for The Mazeway Project.

OUR PREDICAMENT

You and I may agree or disagree about what we see beyond the headlines of our times. Enormous complexity and rapid change make it difficult to grasp a clear picture of where things stand. While it may be a demanding process, all of us should try to resolve our point of view about ourselves and about the world, rather than leaving it to others to shape. Here's an outline of my perception of our situation. You are encouraged to challenge it and express your point of view later, as a participant of The Mazeway Project.

From my point of view, there seems to be no end in sight to the turmoil being experienced within our society and elsewhere on our planet: war, terrorism, environmental challenges, energy crises, poverty, disease, budget deficits, paralyzing debt, a problematic healthcare system, corruption, the effects of globalization, etc. I believe the number is increasing of those who feel that something is seriously wrong. While recognizing that the social process will always be somewhat problematic, I do *not* think a national poll is needed to inform us that an overall negative impression is accruing—an impression that we neither have the vision nor the integrity nor the leadership within our institutions to move us forward constructively.

In the U.S.A. it does not seem to matter who is in the oval office or which party dominates Congress. Nor does it seem to matter which religions prevail or which educational institutions, think tanks, media giants, and special-interest groups have the greatest influence. Somehow, in our embrace of the imperatives of the socio-economic machine of our time, we have managed to institutionalize mediocrity, egocentricity, and duplicity. In government, religion, healthcare, education, business, and in other major institutions, underachievement and incoherence are so pervasive we accept it as normal. While we may be able to point out many positive things, such as empowering technologies, a market economy, political freedom, and an extraordinary institution here and there, our society as a whole has managed to posture itself in a manner that generates more mistrust than confidence, more despair than hope, more chaos than creativity. As a result, we may very well be on the downward slope of the American epoch. Only those in the future looking back will know for sure.

If we are in decline, it is impossible to know all of the consequences. One that is most alarming to me involves young people. I believe they are becoming discouraged about the future, as they try to make sense of a world in constant turmoil—a world with fewer and fewer role models to emulate, and fewer and fewer institutions to respect. This observation alone should remind us that institutions and society as a whole are sustained not only by material and intellectual resources, but also by the trust people have in them. To the degree that trust is diminished, people lose faith and, eventually, if a downward trend should continue, they lose hope. Without trust and hope, chaos ensues.

Regarding adults, as far as I can tell, most of us continue on with our lives as if whatever we may say or do will *not* change things very much. We rely on our leaders to guide us forward, as we try to maintain a positive attitude, thankful and proud of what we and our nation have achieved. At the same time, there are others who argue that we have lost our way—that we should return to traditional precepts. And there are those who believe science and technology will lead the way.

While I appreciate these points of view, I believe we need to be much more inclusive and imaginative. We must develop a comprehensive initiative that honors traditions and respects science, but, at the same time, embraces the reality of a new era challenged by increasing complexity, rapid change globalization, a clash of value systems, and concerns about our environment. I believe no amount of speechmaking, religiosity, nostalgia for the past, scientific breakthrough, or use of political power will generate a viable future, unless the initiative is based on a coherent and moral vision of how we can travel forward together creatively, joyfully, and peacefully as individuals, as a society, and as a species. This overarching vision must transcend our present orientation, which is largely egocentric, provincial, fragmented, and otherwise self-limiting—resulting in behavior that is too often dishonest, hateful, arrogant, and exclusive. Most importantly, the vision must inspire us to design institutions that are self-catalyzing, self-cleansing, and sustainable.

I define a coherent and moral vision as a perspective free of contradictions whose premises would be valid forever. I define self-catalyzing and self-cleansing institutions as those that function organically with checks, balances, and feedback loops that help catalyze and cleanse the system in a manner that spawns creativity, further development, and sustainability. Currently, most institutions function bureaucratically, with traditional top-down organizational structures that lack these attributes.

While not perfect, a good example of an institution that is self-catalyzing and self-cleansing is our democratic form of government. Our founding fathers did an extraordinary job of building checks and balances into the system. However, in spite of their grand vision, our government may not be sustainable, as we have known it, because we have allowed bureaucracy to flourish, and special interest groups to manipulate the levers of power and control to serve narrow interests.

Another example of an institution that incorporates checks and balances is our market economy. The dynamics of supply and demand catalyze and cleanse the system. However, I hasten to add that it works so well that it may not be sustainable because it may drive us mindlessly to consume the resources of the planet faster than they can be renewed.

I do appreciate that many of you may feel I am being too idealistic by suggesting that we need to generate a coherent and moral vision of how we can travel forward together creatively, joyfully, and peacefully; and that the vision must inspire us to design institutions that are self-catalyzing, self-cleansing, and sustainable. But, however lofty this may sound to you, I suspect that anything less will not do, given our predicament. I appeal to those who recognize that the objectives I am suggesting are within our reach if we:

- take a step back from the noise of modernity and realize that it will take time and patience to change what took centuries to entrench;
- collaborate selflessly and creatively;
- establish an educational system that is much more enlightening and empowering;

- sharpen our communication skills to utilize effectively the power of the media and public forums.

Unfortunately, in the absence of such enlightenment, an increasing number of us are becoming disoriented so profoundly that we might not be able to recognize a coherent and moral vision if one were staring back at us. Consequently, confusion prevails, and the fear it generates causes many to retreat to ideologies that claim to offer greater certainty—religious, political, and economic ideologies that magnify differences, spawn hate, and establish the basis for chronic strife.

Why should there be so much disorientation, fear, and a retreat to certainty at a time when so many enjoy the benefits of political freedom, an explosion of new knowledge, empowering technologies, improving living standards, and an awareness of the long view of history? While there is no easy answer to this question, I believe our predicament, more than anything else, is a reflection of our system of education, which is failing its promise, in spite of enormous investments of time and resources.

EDUCATION

Over the centuries the authority of religions diminished, as the State evolved to dominate the social process. In turn, the State's authority gradually diminished, as we began to rely increasingly on our common sense, public opinion, the media, and our conscience to guide us. However, this march toward freedom demanded that we become knowledgeable and learn to think critically and comprehensively if we were to be credible and effective leaders and followers. The need for us to develop in such a manner became, primarily, the responsibility of our system of education, which emerged as the most pivotal institution of the modern age. I wonder, along with an increasing number of other individuals, whether the system is satisfying this role adequately.

As I pressed to gain *an overview* of our system of education, I found myself less interested in detail about this or that part of the system, than being interested in learning whether the system *as a whole* was fulfilling its promise. From my review I concluded that, while our system of education does many things right, it does *not*:

- empower enough of our best and brightest to lead us forward creatively and coherently
- enable most of those who follow to differentiate between truth and lies, reality and illusions
- liberate us from insidious prejudices and self-limiting ideologies

As a result, most of us remain confined within a provincial orientation, unaware of our myopia and our underachievement, and essentially disconnected from the world around us.

Could our system of education overcome such deficiencies? I think so, especially if we look at the challenge from outside the constraints of an incoherent, highly bureaucratized, insular system. From the inside, it is natural to try to "patch" this or that part of the system, rather than question its basic assumptions and design. Consequently, leaders of our educational institutions look, more often than not, to solve *particular* problems. For example, within elementary and secondary education, they focus on budgets, class size, retaining good teachers, parent involvement, textbook selection, union contracts, testing, discipline, etc. In higher education, the focus is on specialization, professional training, and research. While one could argue the importance of each one of these needs, I do *not* think that fulfilling all of them within the prevailing model of education will enable the system to fulfill its promise. If we do not question its basic assumptions and design and respond creatively, educators will continue to fall far short of making the learning process efficient, exciting, and empowering.

Fragmentation

Of all the problems that may exist in our system of education, I believe the most significant is fragmentation. Educators employ curriculums that are so highly fragmented that an objective observer might think there is a conspiracy at work to obfuscate rather than illuminate how the pieces of the puzzles of our existence might fit together. It is only during the earliest years of their education that children are spared the burden of the fragmentation of knowledge.

I think we should accept the reality that curriculum designers have managed to undermine the student's natural inclination and capacity to integrate knowledge. Generations ago, while allowing the allure of industrial-age modeling to rule their sensibilities, they shaped the enterprise of education into a mass-produced commodity. As specialization became the basic organizing technique, educators were driven to put everything in its singular, specific place. The knowledge base was divided with precision into categories and subdivisions, fostering the formation of distinct curricula: Language, Science, Math, Social Studies, etc. This forced teachers to specialize and to function within a top-down, incoherent, self-limiting system of transferring knowledge in schools that, in many cases, function more like factories than learning centers. As a result, our system of education undermines the student's natural drive to integrate knowledge and maximize its use. As more and more data remains disassembled and unintelligible, curiosity is diminished, while the learning process becomes less than exciting, thereby diminishing or stopping altogether the student's desire to comprehend his or her existence holistically. Consequently, instead of becoming oriented comprehensively in our rapidly changing and increasingly complex world, and, instead of becoming adaptable, creative participants in the social process, most students move on with their lives as overspecialized, incidental cogs in one part or another of the mindless socio-economic machine of our time, largely unaware of the premises that empower it, and frustrated about how to adapt to it or how to transform it.

I do not believe we need to commission a panel of experts to affirm these observations. We are immersed in evidence. It is reflected in our disjointed lives, in how long it takes to become full-functioning adults, in how unclear we are about choosing our career, lifestyle, and partners. It is reflected in the measure of our discontent and feeling of powerlessness. Because we are fragmented, we don't know where we are in the mazeway. As a result, we don't have much of a sense of where we are going. More often than not, we submit to someone else's perception about how the world works and our role in it, rather than generate our own point of view.

Of course, focusing on the problem of fragmentation is not unique. As many of us know, there are serious efforts by educators to integrate the curriculum. Core curricula and cultural studies' programs can be pointed to as examples of efforts by some educators to help students "connect the dots" and comprehend things holistically. While such initiatives are worthwhile and should be supported, I do not think they take the process nearly far enough. I say this because I believe that such programs, along with traditional curriculums, lack fundamentally important variables that have been largely overlooked.

Bottom-Up Empowerment

I do not think educators will deal with the problem of fragmentation effectively until they recognize that their top-down methods of transferring knowledge should be combined with empowering bottom-up components.

All of us have experienced the excitement and energy that is generated when someone delivers an interesting lecture or speech. While we may be thrilled by the insights articulated, did you ever wonder what happens to the excitement and energy that was generated? I believe that much of it dissipates within minutes, hours, or days, and, in some instances, the enthusiasm for the insights dissipates completely, as if the event never occurred. I think this is the case because the insights that generated the excitement and energy have no clear place to go - to coalesce, to cohere. We do not have "comprehensive templates" that are designed to enable us to connect the new information with whatever else we know. While we are able to remember information, our mind naturally seeks to integrate disparate elements of knowledge into coherent patterns in an effort to make sense of the world. However, if we are unable to connect new information with the rest of what we know, we simply file it away with the vast amount of other fragments of knowledge that clutter our mind. As a result, the new data may remain useless or be forgotten.

In the next two chapters I introduce Life Mapping and Social Mapping as empowering bottom-up processes driven by comprehensive, open-ended templates. I believe these processes represent the most crucial variable missing from the traditional knowledge-transfer system because they: (1) spawn the integration of the knowledge, and (2) build upon, rather than diminish, students' inherent curiosity about how the world works and how they fit into it.

Life Mapping and Social Mapping are designed for students in school, as well as for those of us who are beyond school years—lifelong learners who choose to stay awake, continue to learn, and make the most of our life. Accordingly, when I refer to students, I am referring to both groups of learners.

IV

LIFE MAPPING

We can't control what others do with
their lives. However, we are free to choose
what we do with our own.

LIFE MAP TEMPLATE

The process of Life Mapping that I propose is empowered by the following 16-point template:

1. Our Opinions about Great Issues
   - The Environment
   - Natural Resources
   - Overpopulation
   - Healthcare
   - Education
   - Leadership
   - Poverty
   - Terrorism
   - Governance
   - Corruption
   - Planned vs. Market Economy
   - Globalization
   - Relativism vs. Absolutism
   - Holistic vs. Myopic Vision
2. Define Our Basic Premises
3. Summarize Our Values & Beliefs
4. Clarify Our Aspirations
5. Survey Our Personality
6. Plan for Further Education
7. Examine Career / Avocation Path
8. Partnering
9. Design Our Lifestyle
10. Define Our Personal Community
11. Define Our Role in the Larger Community
12. Organize Our Financial Plan
13. Accrue Body Wisdom
14. Develop Emotional Wisdom
15. Gain Spiritual Wisdom
16. Write Bio Sketch and/or Maintain a Journal

When we utilize this template to consciously map our life, we benefit in the following manner:

- We have a *clear structure* for organizing our view of ourselves and of the world beyond us.
- We see the *relevancy to us* of the disparate elements of knowledge offered by teachers, books, and our experiences during the course of everyday life.
- We become much more motivated to understand the world because learning has now become a *personal affair*, rather than what may have been largely an impersonal, tedious process of trying to make sense of an endless number of disconnected facts.
- We are encouraged to *take responsibility for our life* based on our own thoughts, feelings, and deep inner

self, thereby enabling us to capture a sense of our true identity, rather than following blindly the identity imposed by the culture around us.

- We feel good about the prospect of developing an increasingly coherent Life Map and an expanding worldview that will enable us to orchestrate an authentic and fulfilling existence as an individual and as part of local and global communities, which we can help make more vibrant and sustainable.

The Process

To help understand this life-mapping process, let's go back in time and remind ourselves how the ancient Greeks tried to deal with the challenge of gaining wisdom.

Socrates employed a process of dialogue to ventilate the great inquiries of his time. He questioned everything through the play of minds, that give-and-take we call "dialectic." (Dialectic may be defined as any formal system of reasoning that arrives at the truth by the exchange of logical arguments.) As you may know, this mode of thought is exemplified and perfected in the dialogues of Plato, whose life was shaped by the teachings of Socrates.

In addition to his writings, Plato established a school in Athens in 387 BC, known as the Academy. The education espoused by Plato was based on the *dialectic technique* Socrates famously advanced. Try to imagine some of the greatest minds of all time (including Aristotle as a student), studying, doing research, and going back and forth challenging one another in pursuit of truth.

With this in mind, let's review the illustration, Comparing Life Maps, and see how it suggests the Socratic Method for energizing the learning process.

Comparing Life Maps

	Life Map 1	Life Map 2	Your Life Map
1. Your Opinion about Great Issues			
The Environment	-- --- ---	-- --- ---	-- --- ---
Natural Resources	-- --- ---	-- --- ---	-- --- ---
Overpopulation	-- --- ---	-- --- ---	-- --- ---
Healthcare	-- --- ---	-- --- ---	-- --- ---
Education	-- --- ---	-- --- ---	-- --- ---
Leadership	-- --- ---	-- --- ---	-- --- ---
Poverty	-- --- ---	-- --- ---	-- --- ---
Terrorism	-- --- ---	-- --- ---	-- --- ---
Governance	-- --- ---	-- --- ---	-- --- ---
Corruption	-- --- ---	-- --- ---	-- --- ---
Planned vs. Market Economies	-- --- ---	-- --- ---	-- --- ---
Globalization	-- --- ---	-- --- ---	-- --- ---
Relativism vs. Absolutism	-- --- ---	-- --- ---	-- --- ---
Holistic vs. Myopic Vision	-- --- ---	-- --- ---	-- --- ---
2. Define Your Basic Premises	-- --- ---	-- --- ---	-- --- ---
3. Summarize Your Values & Beliefs	-- --- ---	-- --- ---	-- --- ---
4. Clarify Your Aspirations	-- --- ---	-- --- ---	-- --- ---
5. Survey Your Personality	-- --- ---	-- --- ---	-- --- ---
6. Plan For Further Education	-- --- ---	-- --- ---	-- --- ---
7. Examine Career/Avocation Path	-- --- ---	-- --- ---	-- --- ---
8. Partnering	-- --- ---	-- --- ---	-- --- ---
9. Design Your Lifestyle	-- --- ---	-- --- ---	-- --- ---
10. Organize a Financial Plan	-- --- ---	-- --- ---	-- --- ---
11. Define Your Personal Community	-- --- ---	-- --- ---	-- --- ---
12. Define Role in Larger Community	-- --- ---	-- --- ---	-- --- ---
13. Accrue Body Wisdom	-- --- ---	-- --- ---	-- --- ---
14. Develop Emotional Wisdom	-- --- ---	-- --- ---	-- --- ---
15. Gain Spiritual Wisdom	-- --- ---	-- --- ---	-- --- ---
16. Write Bio &/or Maintain Journal	-- --- ---	-- --- ---	-- --- ---

The dialectic gets started by reviewing examples of Life Maps. They reveal how other individuals expressed their points of view, and show what completed Life Maps look like. My Life Map is included in Chapter VIII. Other examples can be found on the website, TheMazewayProject.org. You will be able to review them as a departure point for generating your own Life Map.

In addition to reviewing examples, three other activities propel the life-mapping process forward:

1. Readings are suggested that will help flesh out our knowledge of the various subjects involved;
2. There will be give-and-take discussions in the classroom, in small groups in the community, and/or on the Internet that will help us resolve our point of view.
3. There will be a Mazeway Forum on each element of the Life Map Template. You will be free to monitor the interactions among participants and to share your own thoughts and feelings.

The Life Mapping process appears imposing because we are not used to looking at our existence comprehensively in a step-by-step manner. And we may not be able to imagine how the process could be introduced in a highly simplified manner during the early years of the educational process. It is much easier to imagine how it could be introduced to college students and to those of us beyond college years.

Since we are trying to chart our life holistically, we should keep in mind that Life Mapping is a not a trivial exercise. We should take the time necessary to complete a first draft. At that point we will appreciate that the mapping process is a lifelong affair, since we continue to learn and grow and change. What could be more important than gaining an overall sense of who we are and how we can orchestrate an authentic, satisfying life?

In addition to being factual, our other challenge will be to reconcile the variables of our entire Life Map in a manner that is free of contradictions. For example, regarding the issue of

The Environment, if we feel that consumers should be more disciplined to help preserve the environment, we would be caught in a contradiction if we reveal in the Lifestyle segment of our Life Map that we prefer to drive an SUV that is *unnecessarily* large. Being free of contradictions becomes especially important when it comes to premises, values, and beliefs, and how they relate to what is said elsewhere within one's Life Map. Once we deal successfully with the challenge of being both factual and coherent, we can proceed with our lives as authentic persons, rather than those who conform thoughtlessly to conventional wisdom.

We are free to add to the list of great issues and to the other elements of the template. And, we are encouraged to go beyond the reading suggestions, since the combination offered may not be inclusive enough for us. Regarding the sample Life Maps, we will realize that they are simply examples of how other people expressed their point of view. For our personal use, we will be free to utilize the language expressed within the examples. Assuming we will be using a computer to assemble our Life Map, we will be able to download and copy, cut and paste, assemble and reassemble in any manner, and from any source that helps us resolve positions that best reflect our point of view. Most importantly, since the various exercises are intended to help us arrive at *our truth*, we would be free to challenge everything, including the template itself.

Dare To Be Great

Such an open-ended, safe, learning environment supports the premise that the individual represents the basic unit of the social process, the authentic carrier of reality, not our institutions per se. If not enough of us get our own life together and dare to be great, we should expect that our institutions will.

I believe most of us, who experience the process of Life Mapping, will feel empowered by it and wonder why we were not encouraged during our many years in school to map our life in a systematic manner. We will realize that consciously mapping our life prompts us to be more independent-minded and to think more critically. As a result, we will feel better prepared to be credible and effective leaders and followers. If these predictions are affirmed, the process of Life Mapping will eventually become an integral part of school curricula and help transform our system of education in a manner that makes it more efficient, more exciting, and more empowering.

I think it is important to point out that, actually, the goal of education has always been to enable students to develop a more holistic, more integrated view of themselves and of the complexities of society and the human condition. With this perspective in mind, the Life Mapping process I am suggesting can be seen as an important step in the fulfillment of education's long-established promise. The Mazeway Project does indeed challenge the education establishment to acknowledge that its integrative role is increasingly being compromised in an ever more fragmented and over-specialized system. The solution advanced here is only radical in the literal sense of that word, as it prods educators to return to the root or "radix" of education's purpose. Aristotle, by insisting that his students examine first causes and the nature of things, for example, was not rejecting the pursuit of practical knowledge in favor of integrative knowledge; he was instead embracing both. It is precisely within this spirit that the Life Mapping process enables students to integrate their knowledge into a coherent view of themselves and of the world, while they continue to acquire the practical and specialized knowledge they will need to enter the workforce in a highly productive way. Life Mapping, therefore, is a complementary process to today's educational system.

I think it is also worth mentioning that, at this time, a great amount of energy and resources are being applied to the No Child Left Behind program. While we may appreciate the good intentions of this program, what is not being recognized sufficiently, if at all, is that our system of education leaves behind most of our best and brightest students when measured by: (1) how well they integrate the knowledge they accrued, and (2) how coherently they are oriented in our increasingly complex, rapidly changing, information-saturated world. The more gifted students are largely ignored in these terms because it is assumed that they "get it." While this may be true in a relative sense, I do not think it is true when measured by the criteria mentioned above. The consequence of this illusion may be significant because we depend on our best and brightest to lead us forward, including devising the most effective methods of educating those we have been leaving behind.

V

SOCIAL MAPPING

The history of mankind is strewn with habits,
creeds, and dogma that were essential
to one age and disastrous in another.

- JAMES RESTON

SOCIAL MAPS

In the previous chapter I explained how Life Mapping enables us to gain an overall sense of who we are and how we can orchestrate an authentic, satisfying life as an individual. Social Mapping, on the other hand, directs our attention *beyond ourselves*, toward generating coherent Social Maps that help us actualize our best possibilities as a society.

To be oriented in our society, we follow Social Maps advanced by our family and by various religious, educational, governmental, and economic institutions. They prescribe values and beliefs, how we are to be educated and governed, the rules of the marketplace, etc.

Unfortunately, we have not been prepared very well to question the assumptions and effectiveness of established Social Maps, since we have been nurtured primarily to conform. As a result we follow one set of maps or another, more or less blindly, while ignoring the possibility of adopting more inclusive and more powerful Social Maps. While the world around us may be coming unhinged, we conclude there must be something wrong with the maps of others that are leading to problems. We remain unaware that the Social Maps we subscribe to can enhance our development or undermine it; they can liberate us or imprison us. This applies to us individually and collectively, which is why the processes of Life Mapping and Social Mapping go hand in hand. We need both.

As things stand today, an increasing number of us wonder whether our institutions are fulfilling their role adequately. We feel disillusioned by incompetence, malfeasance, and incoherence. At the same time, we feel powerless and disconnected without the means of relating effectively to countless other individuals who also feel dissatisfied and frustrated with the status quo.

The strategy here is to view the social process holistically and to learn to connect with one another in a manner that: (1) enables us to become active, creative players in the human drama; and (2) increases the chances of generating more positive outcomes.

THE SOCIAL PROCESS

To begin Social Mapping on solid ground, I suggest that we grasp an *overview* of the social process and its dynamics before we focus on particular parts. In other words, instead of focusing on political, economic, or cultural aspects, and running the risk of getting sidetracked or lost in detail, we will first capture an overall sense of how these dimensions of the social process relate to one another.

I suspect most of us use the term, "social process," without having a clear idea how to define it. Accordingly, I thought Figure 1. might be useful to you.

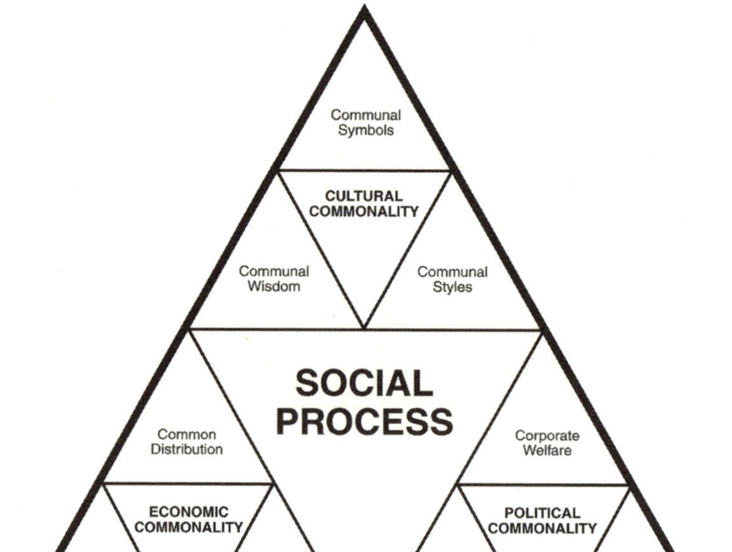

Figure 1. The Social Process

The triangular modeling suggests that the combination of our economic, political, and cultural institutions constitutes the social process.

- Cultural institutions deal with communal symbols, wisdom, and styles.
- Economic institutions deal with resources, production, and distribution.
- Political institutions deal with order, justice, and welfare.

Each one of the three kinds of institutions is essential to the other two. Our economic institutions support our political and cultural institutions. Without viability in this sector, we cannot sustain very well our political and cultural institutions. In turn, our political institutions provide order and protect the others, while our cultural institutions provide meaning for our economic institutions, and shed light on the political processes. It is this complementary relationship among them that makes possible a viable society.

It is important to note that, when one sector of the social process dominates the other two, a state of imbalance exists. This can have far-reaching consequences.

For example, many of us believe we are living at a time when economic considerations prevail. Propelled by breakthroughs in science and technology, and benefiting from the dynamics of a market economy, our economic institutions have accumulated enormous power and influence over our political and cultural institutions. As a result they skew the dynamics of the social process. We find education becoming a mass-produced commodity—a part of the "knowledge industry" which prepares us to fill a niche in the socio-economic machine. Families come under economic pressure as a result of clever marketing techniques which generate social imperatives that encourage unnecessary consumption and cause paralyzing debt. Our healthcare system's effectiveness is diminished by the economic self-interests of insurance companies, hospitals, practitioners, and drug companies.

Financial considerations affect politics so pervasively it might be difficult to find politicians who are not unduly influenced by PACs and special-interests' contributions, and/or tainted otherwise by some kind of malfeasance. With a perverse focus on profits, executives of many businesses violate the interests of their stakeholder and the general public. Our media, the wild card in the social process, are often ruled by the bottom line, rather than by the imperative of seeking and presenting the truth. If that were not enough, many of us believe that our environment is becoming a casualty of economic forces.

Figure 2. illustrates the Distortion of the Social Process when economic considerations prevail.

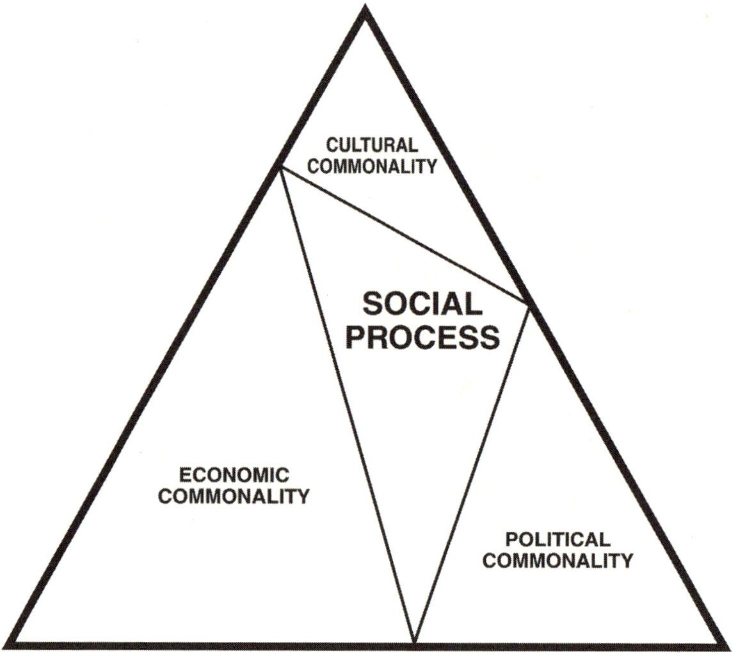

Figure 2. Distortion of the Social Process

On the other hand, our political institutions distort the social process when they, less than perfectly if not corruptly, conceive and orchestrate policies that affect healthcare, banking, commerce, taxes, foreign affairs, the military, justice, the media, insurance, the environment, and other dimensions of our existence. One could argue that the pervasive influence and questionable practices of our political institutions skew the social process more than economic institutions do.

And then there are our cultural institutions, which are primarily the family, religion, education, and the arts. We find that they can skew the social process by underachieving in their role to provide meaning, purpose, and a sense of morality to our lives. When they underachieve, our economic and political institutions will flounder.

Agreement regarding what's in a state of imbalance and who is responsible is not as important at this point as understanding that the social process is hardly ever in balance. Unless we are mindful that disequilibrium among our institutions can generate consequences and unless we consciously work toward trying to keep the social process in balance, we run the risk of disassembling into chaos and becoming yet another failed culture. At the same time, I recognize that one could argue that positive outcomes can ensue if one sector of the social process dominates the other two in a highly moral and creative manner. While I appreciate that position, I believe there would be a greater likelihood of positive outcomes over the long run when the social process is in a state of equilibrium.

To help us view the social process holistically and progress forward constructively, I introduce here a Social Map Template.

SOCIAL MAP TEMPLATE

As you see, the template on the next page divides the major aspects of the social process into three major categories, Cultural Constructs, Economic Constructs, and Political Constructs. And then it prompts us to compare examples of the various elements of Social Maps. For MetaVision and Religion, the examples for comparison might be descriptions of Judaism,

The Template

	Social Map Examples	My Social Map	Our Social Map
CULTURAL CONSTRUCTS			
MetaVision	-- --- ---	-- --- ---	-- --- ---
Religion	-- --- ---	-- --- ---	-- --- ---
Family	-- --- ---	-- --- ---	-- --- ---
Education	-- --- ---	-- --- ---	-- --- ---
Science	-- --- ---	-- --- ---	-- --- ---
Information/Knowledge	-- --- ---	-- --- ---	-- --- ---
Healthcare	-- --- ---	-- --- ---	-- --- ---
Media	-- --- ---	-- --- ---	-- --- ---
Social Networks	-- --- ---	-- --- ---	-- --- ---
The Arts	-- --- ---	-- --- ---	-- --- ---
ECONOMIC CONSTRUCTS			
Technological Resources	-- --- ---	-- --- ---	-- --- ---
Natural Resources	-- --- ---	-- --- ---	-- --- ---
Human Resources	-- --- ---	-- --- ---	-- --- ---
Production Systems	-- --- ---	-- --- ---	-- --- ---
Consumption Plans	-- --- ---	-- --- ---	-- --- ---
Exchange Mechanisms	-- --- ---	-- --- ---	-- --- ---
Property Claims	-- --- ---	-- --- ---	-- --- ---
POLITICAL CONSTRUCTS			
Corporate Welfare	-- --- ---	-- --- ---	-- --- ---
Corporate Order	-- --- ---	-- --- ---	-- --- ---
Corporate Justice	-- --- ---	-- --- ---	-- --- ---

Christianity, Islam, Buddhism, and Taoism. Within the various Economic Constructs, the examples might be descriptions of various elements of a Planned Economy, a Market Economy, and a Hybrid Economy. We are free to identify with any combination of positions. Whatever we choose, we would assemble our own positions to form what we will call My Social Map. In doing so, we imply that our combination of positions represents the Social Map we advance personally as being the most enabling.

However, the Social Mapping process does not stop there. It goes on to challenge us to work with others to generate what is labeled Our Social Map – a challenge to compose a perspective that the class or other group of individuals agree upon collectively. Ideally, this would be a perspective that is more inclusive and more empowering.

As in the case of Life Mapping, two other activities propel forward the Social Mapping process: (1) readings are suggested that will help flesh out our knowledge of the various subjects involved; and (2) there will be give-and-take discussions within classrooms, in small groups in the community, and/or on the Internet that will help us clarify our point of view, individually and collectively.

Within this open-ended, collaborative process, we are challenged to: (a) be factual; (b) transcend our differences; and (c) reconcile the variables within the maps in a manner that is absent of contradictions and that leads to institutions that are self-catalyzing, self-cleansing, and sustainable. In the most idealistic sense, the process of Social Mapping challenges us to realize what is possible and noble for our society and for the human race.

Once again, we are free to go beyond the reading suggestions, since the combination offered may not be inclusive enough. Assuming that we will be using a computer to assemble the Social Maps, we will be able to download and copy, cut and paste, assemble and reassemble in any manner, and from any source that helps us resolve positions that best reflect our perceptions. Most importantly, since the various exercises are intended to help us arrive, individually and collectively, at what we think is the most enabling perspective, we would be free to challenge everything, including the template itself.

LIFE + SOCIAL MAPPING

Those of us who may have already begun Life Mapping come into the process of Social Mapping with greater interest in the outcomes of the social process. We realize that we can't fulfill the best possibilities of our life if we are encumbered by dysfunctional institutions. Therefore, we are curious to find out what within the social process supports or stands in the way of our opinions, needs, and aspirations.

As we proceed, we discover that our opinions about Great Issues represent a framework for how we will engage the process of Social Mapping. Our opinions reveal an orientation of how we will direct our lives within the community, including how we will vote and what we would do if we were in charge. Of course we realize that our opinions may change as a result of interacting with others, and as a result of studying further the subtleties and complexities of the social process. Our opinions may also change as a result of real-life experiences.

The combination of Life Mapping and Social Mapping prompts us to: (1) think more critically, (2) rise above the malleable masses, and (3) utilize more fully our capacity to envision viable futures for ourselves and for humankind.

OUR NICHE IN THE SOCIAL PROCESS

As individuals within the social process, we can function as malleable, incidental props or as curious, creative participants. We are props to the degree we remain passive and unaware. We are creative participants to the degree we pursue our life's journey consciously and imaginatively.

Here is my perception of the reach of our minds and hearts within the social process and beyond, as we struggle, individually and collectively, to resolve our identity and fulfill our best possibilities.

General Masses

Please examine Figure 3. It suggests that most of us are part of the General Masses. As such, we are highly malleable. That is to say our minds and hearts can be shaped and perhaps reshaped by the programs of the mind espoused by our institutions, for better or worse.

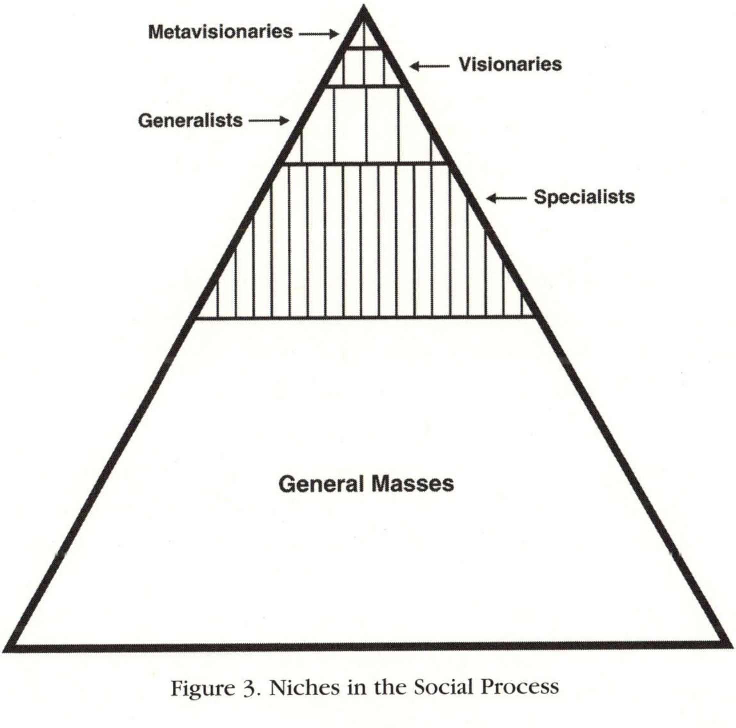

Figure 3. Niches in the Social Process

Specialists

As you will note, the diagram positions Specialists above the General Masses. Fewer in number, Specialists include scientists, physicians, lawyers, jurists, accountants, teachers, scholars, economists, politicians, priests, ministers, and rabbis, along with experts in other fields. Specialists can be highly useful to us because their programs embody knowledge and skills that may help us deal with one aspect or another of our lives. Specialists may also hurt us if their narrow focus happens to be faulty, or leaves out important variables relevant to the challenge at hand. Of course, Specialists seek advice from other Specialists, and they are also malleable, more or less, like the rest of us.

I think we are used to differentiating ourselves in these terms. We readily understand and accept the role of Specialists in the social process. Less common is appreciating the role of Generalists.

Generalists

Fewer in number than Specialists, Generalists function at a higher level of integration than most Specialists can achieve. Either by training or by natural inclination they are able to discern the connections among a wider range of disparate elements of knowledge and of organizational structure. Their unique attribute, which is difficult to measure, gives them the capacity to capture a sense of the big picture—to see things more holistically. They know intuitively the strategic questions that should be asked, while having the wherewithal otherwise to orchestrate a complex array of political and operational variables. In short supply, Generalists are more likely to become the managers within, or leaders of, our institutions, and, as a result, gain more power and earn more money than those in the groups below.

A Generalist does not need to have been a Specialist. However, being highly specialized may make it difficult for him or her to generalize creatively.

At the same time, it is important to recognize that some individuals may employ the attributes of a generalist in a manner that is destructive. Accordingly, we may refer to them as Destructive Generalists, whereas others may be called

Creative Generalists. While we will emphasize the positive here, we must keep in mind the presence of both life-affirming and life-negating inclinations, as humans make choices during their journey in the mazeway.

Generalists include leaders in religion, education, politics, government, business, the military, and in other institutions. They can be highly effective during their entire lifetime, unless a new paradigm comes along that demands adaptation to change. I suspect relatively few Generalists have the capacity to adapt to major paradigm shifts. Those who do can be characterized as Visionaries.

Visionaries

Figure 3. shows the position of Visionaries relative to Generalists, Specialists, and the General Masses. As the diagram suggests, Visionaries are very few in number. These are highly gifted individuals who evolve to a level of awareness, if not a level of morality, beyond those in the strata below. By their nature, and perhaps somewhat by training, they have a much greater sense of how the *larger features* of the big picture fit together. As you would expect, they are more likely to have been Generalists than simply Specialists. Somehow, as established paradigms become exhausted of their energy, Visionaries are able to discern coherent patterns within what appears to others to be mostly chaos. Or they may simply perceive a better way of doing something that is still working satisfactorily. Examples of visionaries from my point of view include: Galileo, Leonardo da Vinci, Sir Isaac Newton, Baruch Spinoza, Charles Darwin, Thomas Edison, Henry Ford, Teihard de Chardin, Mahatma Gandhi, Nelson Mandela, and the Dalai Lama. In the flux of the social process, Visionaries express their godlike (creative) faculties, and, depending on the times and the circumstances, may have a dramatic effect for years to come on the lives of the General Masses, as well as on the lives of Specialists and Generalists.

While some Visionaries have a positive effect and may be referred to as Creative Visionaries, others, such as Adolph Hitler, Joseph Stalin, and Osama Bin Laden, have a destructive effect, as if expressing devil-like faculties. They may be as intelligent and insightful as the Creative Visionaries mentioned above, except they resort to the dark side of their nature, generating entropy instead of creative energy. We may refer to them as Destructive Visionaries.

It is important to note that an individual need not change the course of history, or be famous otherwise, to be considered a Visionary. I believe there have probably been countless thousands of individuals through the ages with the attributes of a Visionary who may have functioned creatively or destructively, but remain obscure. I suspect most Visionaries are rejected because they are perceived as being strange, crazy, and/or present a threat to established institutions.

MetaVisonaries

And then there are the MetaVisionaries, whom we may call prophets, shamans, and mystics. As extraordinary as they are rare, these individuals are positioned at the very top of the hierarchy of humankind's mental and spiritual capacities.

It seems that MetaVisionaries not only possess the attributes of Visionaries; they are also able to access the mind of God *within* them as well as the mind of God *beyond* them, as if there were no distinction. At least that is how it may be perceived by the MetaVisionary and/or by his or her interpreters and, in turn, by those who follow.

While all of us may possess godlike attributes, MetaVisionaries have the capacity to function *as God* per se, if only as an intermediary. It's as though they reached *the* top of the mountain and were able to perceive an endless horizon and beyond in a seamless, integral manner, and feel an inherent part of it all, if only fleetingly. In my opinion, examples of MetaVisionaries include Socrates, Jesus, Mohammed, The Buddha, and Albert Einstein.

My purpose here is to explain the phenomenon of MetaVisionaries the best I can to shed light on what I think are the highest mental, social, and spiritual attributes humans may possess. It is through these attributes that our view of the mazeway is illuminated the most.

I believe the potential to become a MetaVisionary and fulfill our godlike attributes is inherent in more of us than we realize. Whether or not that potential is fulfilled depends as much on the vagaries of our cultural environment as it does on our will to transcend what may appear to be our limitations.

FREE TO CHOOSE

We specialize; we generalize; we envision; and some may see forever beyond the horizon. These exercises of mind and heart shape our being, individually and collectively. What we become, what we actualize or not, *depends on the choices we make*—on how well we orchestrate our consciousness to satisfy physical, psychological, and spiritual needs.

Up to now, the social process has been a haphazard affair, like an unending series of experiments to test humankind's capacity to adapt and to create. Through the ages, countless societal failures were followed by other strategies, few in number,which generated extraordinary cultures. Some of them prevailed for many centuries, but, unfortunately, they would not satisfy the fuller test of time. As we look back and examine the remnants of their achievements, we wonder what went wrong—why a pattern of remarkable development and creativity would ultimately be overshadowed by a precipitous or gradual decline.

A casual glance at this pattern may suggest that humans embody a flaw that eventually manifests itself within the institutions we design to fulfill the visions we become compelled to follow. It's as if a life-negating tendency inevitably wins out over a life-affirming tendency as we choose paths in the mazeway that lead to dishonest, hateful, egocentric, arrogant, and exclusive behavior. It's as if we manage to delude ourselves and incorporate within our institutions enough of our dark side to make them unable, sooner or later, to deal with the winds of change and to reconcile with enemies at the gate. It's as if we allow ignorance to prevail over any wisdom we accrue, as we brazenly impose our will and our certainty on each other.

A further review of the historical pattern suggests that a lack of foresight may have been at work, as much as any moral flaw. Our ancestors did not know the long-term consequences of the choices they were making. They did not have, as we do, the benefit of an historical overview of programs of the mind that empowered institutions - programs that would ultimately fail. They did not have extensive science, technology, and other modern resources, including a view of our planet from outer space and a sense of quantum physics to provide perspective.

Today, therefore, we should know better than those who came before us. We should be able to develop programs that enable us to direct our lives intelligently, while recognizing that the sum of what we think and feel, and what we do or do not do will affect the outcome of this chapter of the human drama and the chapters that follow.

CHALLENGING QUESTIONS

I do not present examples of Social Maps within this book because they should be created out of an illuminating dialectic. The website, TheMazewayProject.org, will provide examples of Social Maps that students and others assemble.

Whether the dialectic takes place within a classroom, a group setting at home, or online, participants will be encouraged to generate Social Maps that respond constructively to a wide range of demanding questions drawn from the disciplines of philosophy, anthropology, religion, sociology, history, political science, and economics. Questions, such as:

- If prejudices, illusions, and self-limiting ideologies pervade the social process, what can we do about it?
- Do all people have the same power for change? If not, what gives some people more power than others?
- Besides people, what are the main actors or structures in the social environment? At what level do they operate? E.g., neighborhood, national, international.
- What about the market? Is it an important force or structure? What about government?
- What social factors most shape our personalities?
- What are some of the main forces that operate in the social process? E.g., norms, traditions, resources, authority.
- If enough resources exist to feed the world's population, why do we allow so many people to die of hunger? And, why do so many people die of diseases for which there is a cure?
- If bureaucracies underachieve and usually fail in the long run, why do we continue to bureaucratize our institutions?
- What social forces are most likely to stand in the way of achieving our aspirations as individuals and our aspirations as a group? What social forces will help achieve them?

Of all the questions that should be included on this list, I think the most important is:

- Do we have the wherewithal to stop the endless cycle of misadventures, destruction, and despair by conceptualizing a coherent and moral vision of how we can move forward together creatively, joyfully, and peacefully?

I keep raising this question because I believe it points to the crux of humankind's quandary as a species. Either we respond to the challenge successfully, or we risk a highly problematic, if not a disastrous future. We can begin the process of formulating such a vision by focusing our attention on the very first element of the Social Map Template, i.e. MetaVision, which is the subject of the next chapter.

VI

METAVISIONING

A new, physically uncompromised initiative
of unbiased integrity could unify the world.[18]

– R. BUCKMINSTER FULLER

OUR CHALLENGE AS A SPECIES

I ended the previous chapter asking what is probably the most demanding question facing humankind as a species. It is interesting to note that those who are pragmatic feel that it is useless to ask such a question. When challenged, they respond indifferently. And there are those who remain silent, surprised that someone is so idealistic to ask, given the complexity of our times. In the wake of such apathy, the human drama continues, as if left to the gods to script.

To capture a sense of the scope of the challenge we face, consider the following six stories that Walter Turett Anderson summarized in his illuminating book, *REALTY Isn't What It Used To Be.*[1] He characterized these global stories as "attempts to explain the world - to create a new global reality - and attempts to further the aspirations, hopes, political agendas, and ego needs of different groups of people."

1. The Western myth of progress, with its enthusiasm for technological change and economic development and its overriding image of a world in which the conditions of life keep getting better for everybody.

2. The Marxist story of revolution and international socialism.

3. The Christian fundamentalist story about a return to a society governed by the basis of Christian values and biblical belief.

4. The Islamic fundamentalist story about the return to a society governed on the basis of Islamic values and koranic belief.

5. The Green story about rejecting the myth of progress and governing societies according to ecological values.

6. The "new paradigm" story about a sudden leap forward to a new way of being and a new way of understanding the world.

Mr. Anderson noted that these six stories were "not meant to be a complete inventory, but rather an exploratory description of some ways that people are trying to make sense of the postmodern world." He goes on to explain that, whatever permutation of such global stories one might promote, they all fail one way or another to provide an inclusive and coherent vision of how to deal comprehensively and effectively with our highly problematic reality. Even the new paradigm story fails to "tell us much about what to do in a world that has lots of paradigms, and lots of paradigms about paradigms, and any number of stories claiming to be the key to the future." He concludes: "These competing ideologies will be part of global civilization, but, at least in their more fundamental aspects, will be more forces for divisiveness than for unification. We have to look beyond them for clues as to what may hold a maturing postmodern civilization together."

Mr. Anderson summarizes humankind's challenge very well. However, I believe it would be a mistake to think simply in terms of what may "hold" a maturing postmodern civilization together. We must do much more than that, if we are to survive the strong possibility that postmodernism represents a dead-end in the mazeway. We must realize that the confluence of premodern, modern, and postmodern orientations within what is becoming our "global village," has set the stage for serious conflicts, if not disaster. This is not a predication of what's to come. We are already experiencing it. Consequently, we are challenged to generate a more inclusive vision of our reality that will lead us forward creatively as individuals, as societies, and as a species. I believe the first step toward generating such a vision is to appreciate more fully the simple fact that our future depends on a combination of (a) how well we design and orchestrate our institutions, and (b) on how we choose to orchestrate our lives as individuals. Accordingly, the future is in our hands to shape, not left to the gods to script – unless we mean the god inherent within us.

EGOCENTRIC INSTITUTIONS

A major part of our reality is that we have many deeply entrenched institutions that are dedicated to perpetuating their power and control, along with their agenda and ideological preferences, whether or not their programs add to the viability of our species. I believe this is due primarily to the fact that very few of them are designed to be self-catalyzing and self-cleansing. While the premises and values of the vision that spawned an institution may be worthwhile, the institution eventually matures and may become so highly bureaucratized and insular that it undermines creativity, rejects new knowledge that challenges its programs, and, sometimes, even violates the premises and values on which the institution was founded. This is true of most religious, governmental, educational, and health-care institutions, as well as business, labor-union, and social-service institutions. As such, most of them will fight to affirm their programs. There may be talented leaders and imaginative staff members involved in the orchestration of the institutions. However, without organizational mechanisms in place to catalyze and cleanse them, the institutions stumble along as clumsy, incoherent, ineffective, and sometimes menacing giants until a major crisis comes along that demands change. When such egocentric behavior by major institutions dominates the social process, the society runs the risk of crumbling.

CONCEPTUAL IMPRISONMENT

How we choose to orchestrate our lives as individuals also relates directly to the challenge humankind faces to survive as a species.

It is important to be reminded that most of us follow one set of programs of the mind or another, as a result of the accident of the time and place of birth, our family's orientation, and the prescriptions and proscriptions advanced by the prevailing institutions around us. As I mentioned before, the programs we follow are so commanding that most of us are not inclined to question them. We simply seek affirmation of what we already believe. Consequently, we allow ourselves to be conceptually imprisoned by illusions, prejudices, and self-limiting ideologies propagated by institutions, while ignoring the possibility of adopting a more inclusive and a more empowering perspective. By following blindly the prescriptions and proscriptions advanced by institutions, we help perpetuate their power and control, whether or not it is deserved.

The *combination* of our conceptual imprisonment and the egocentricity of our institutions suggests that the challenge humankind faces is *systemic*. As such, a fundamental shift in our consciousness is required, rather than tactical efforts to patch this or that *part* of the system. I believe the shift in our consciousness should begin with an emphasis on empowering us as individuals to function as whole, critically-thinking, creative participants of the social process, rather than remaining imprisoned within a twilight zone of awareness in which we delude ourselves we are oriented and free in the mazeway. Accordingly, I do not think we should depend solely on our institutions to bring about a shift in our consciousness.

CONCEPTUAL FREEDOM

We as individuals should be accepted as the true and authentic carriers of reality,[28] not our institutions. Institutions do not generate new ideas and visions. They incorporate the new ideas and visions that *individuals* conceive, and, more often than not, fail to fulfill the promise of those ideas and visions. It is we who think, feel, intuit, imagine, and create, and who possess a moral compass that enables us to navigate the mazeway. It is institutions that perpetuate prejudices, illusions, and self-limiting ideologies by programming each new generation to follow their prescriptions and proscriptions. The flaws within those prescriptions and proscriptions are not inherent within our being; they are taught to us.

When we understand that we are a reflection of our institutions and they are a reflection of us, we realize that our lack of an overview and of creative participation in the social process allows institutions to bureaucratize senselessly, consolidate power and control, and, ultimately, ossify, while we remain fragmented, alienated, and polarized. Once we gain this perspective and escape our conceptual imprisonment, we become more hopeful because we know that some combination of us has the wherewithal to generate an overarching vision of how we can move forward together more constructively.

While this perception of our situation may be over-simplified, I believe it helps explain: (1) why humankind has been experiencing an endless cycle of misadventures, destruction, and despair; (2) why no major civilization has survived the test of time, and (3) why we should not expect from any of our major institutions the coherent and moral leadership we need.

GENERATING A NEW METAVISION

In the Social Mapping chapter, I discussed MetaVisionaries – those unusual individuals we call prophets, shamans, and mystics. As examples, I mentioned: Socrates, Jesus, Mohammed, The Buddha, and Albert Einstein. Unfortunately, we do not have a *contemporary* MetaVisionary, someone with sufficient foresight, universality, integrity, and clarity to guide us through and beyond the turmoil of postmodern times. Given our predicament, I suggest that, instead of waiting for a MetaVisionary to come along, we should work together to generate an overarching perspective ourselves through a special kind of collaboration that will amplify our *combined* wisdom and creativity.

Most of us are familiar with forums, chat rooms, and blogging. Not as many are familiar with "open-source collaboration" on the Internet. The open-source movement is described by Thomas L. Friedman in his book,[15] *The World Is Flat*, as follows: "…it involves thousands of people around the world coming together online to collaborate in writing everything from their own software to their own operating systems to their own dictionary to their own recipe for cola—building always from the bottom up rather than accepting formats or content imposed by corporate hierarchies from the top down. Open-source software is shared, constantly improved by its users, and made available for free to anyone. In return, every user who comes up with an improvement—a patch that makes this software sing or dance better—is encouraged to make the patch available to every other user for free."

Examples of this global phenomenon are: (1) Linux, the popular computer operating system that competes with Microsoft's Windows; and (2) Wikipedia, a free-content encyclopedia, written collaboratively by people from around the world.

The Mazeway Project utilizes open-source collaboration to catalyze the process of MetaVisioning – the quest to generate an overarching perspective that illuminates our way forward. There are four major steps involved in the process:

1. Become clearly aware of our *present* thoughts and feelings about ourselves and the world around us by developing our Life Map.
2. Enter the MetaVisioning process accepting the fact that collaborators come from a diverse range of cultural orientations. We must be prepared to listen and question until all of the participants feel their basic premises, needs, and aspirations are understood, if not agreed upon.
3. Patiently search for common treads in the premises of the various cultural orientations, understanding that it's the primary premises that empower the programs of the mind that frame our own orientation and that of the other participants. The basic challenge collaborators face as a group is resolve a coherent and moral set of premises about our reality that are truly universal and empowering, rather than accepting premises that may be provincial and self-limiting.
4. Based on the clarity we gain from the first three steps of this process, we are prepared to begin dealing with the challenge of generating an overarching MetaVision of how we can move forward together creatively, joyfully, and peacefully.

It is hoped that, if such a coherent and moral perspective materializes, it will be based on *universal premises* that: (a) embrace the needs and aspirations of all humankind, (b) incorporate what is known about matter, life, and mind, and (c) spawn self-catalyzing and self-cleansing social constructs that would break the endless cycle of misadventures, destruction, and despair that humankind has been enduring.

To get the MetaVisioning process started, I will post on the website (TheMazewayProject.org) my Life Map, which includes my page-zero premises. (You will find it here within Chapter VIII.) In the spirit of open-source collaboration, you and the other participants are invited to *challenge, correct, or displace* everything I suggest in an effort to generate a more inclusive and coherent perspective. It is important to keep in mind that this process is not about *my* premises and perspective or your premises and perspective; it is about *OUR* premises and perspective.

Another important part to getting the collaboration started is to establish a safe and open learning environment that is imbued with humility, compassion, and trust. It will not surprise me that within such an environment there will be individuals who come forward with transcendent insights that lead to a new MetaVison. They will be uncommon individuals who: (a) emerged from the malleable masses, (b) avoided the pitfalls of over-specialization and self-limiting ideologies, (c) are able to generalize and envision better than the rest of us, and (d) are somehow able to perceive our reality in an integral manner, if only fleetingly.

I do appreciate that this is a very abstract, demanding process. And, while it may take time to generate a new MetaVision, the process itself will expand our awareness and empower us to function as critically thinking, sovereign citizens of the mazeway, rather than submissive cogs in the socio-economic machine of our time.

If a new MetaVision materializes from this process, I hope it is *not* institutionalized in a manner that future generations might follow blindly. The MetaVision should be utilized in an open-ended, self-catalyzing, and self-cleansing manner that illuminates humankind's developmental journey in the mazeway.

CLARITY AND HOPE

I believe the combination of Life Mapping, Social Mapping, and MetaVisioning will lead us to greater clarity and hope regarding how to fulfill our best possibilities as individuals, as a culture, and as a species. We improve the chances of this happening when we connect with one another and utilize the dialectic method of dialogue dedicated to subordinating our ego while being compassionate and loving. Within such an illuminating environment, we can learn more than we ever thought possible:

1. We learn to differentiate self-limiting ideologies from those that are open-ended and adaptive.
2. We recognize prejudices that diminish us and illusions that mislead us.
3. We gain our true identity, rather than retain, without questioning it, an identity resulting from the accident of the time and place of birth, our family's orientation, and other influences of the socio-cultural setting of our situation.
4. We escape the twilight zone of awareness where our ignorance and disconnection from one another help perpetuate systems of power and control that divide us more than they enable us to work together to build better social constructs that satisfy the needs of all humankind.
5. We understand why highly bureaucratized institutions generate more entropy than creativity and underachieve, if not fail ultimately, while institutions that are self-catalyzing and self-cleansing spawn creativity, further development, and sustainability.
6. We appreciate how the effects of rapid change, increasing complexity, and globalization overwhelm

us, pressing many to retreat fearfully to positions of certainty and closure, rather than choosing to explore the frontiers of mind and heart, and the mazeway beyond.

7. We learn how to diminish discordance among humans, and replace it with a greater awareness that we are all one species with the capacity to reconcile our differences and evolve to the next level of our developmental journey.

VII

MAZEWAY WEBSITE

Powerful online resources
illuminate and extend the processes of
Life Mapping, Social Mapping, and MetaVisioning.

THEMAZEWAYPROJECT.ORG

The most empowering resource of this project is its website, TheMazewayProject.org. Under construction, the website is envisioned to be an open-ended, information utility that will enable visitors to participate: (1) on their own, (2) as part a group activity, or (3) through courses offered by schools in traditional classroom situations or through the processes of Distance Learning. In addition to Life Mapping, Social Mapping, and MetaVisioning, visitors will be invited to participate in Mazeway Forums and in Mazeway Networking. Here's how the primary elements of The Mazeway Project are described on the website.

Life Mapping: Empowered by a 16-point Life Map Template, this process enables us to gain an overall sense of who we are as an individual and how we can orchestrate an authentic, satisfying, healthy life.

Social Mapping directs our attention beyond ourselves toward generating coherent Social Maps that help us envision how to build vibrant and sustainable institutions and communities.

MetaVisioning: invites us to participate in a worldwide, open-source collaboration dedicated to achieving an overarching vision of how humankind can move forward together creatively, joyfully, and peacefully.

Mazeway Forums provide the opportunity to interact with others concerning the various aspects of Life Mapping and Social Mapping.

Mazeway Networks connect individuals and groups on the basis of common interests and aspirations.

VIII

MY LIFE MAP

What follows is my own Life Map.
It represents an example of how the
Life Map Template can be utilized.
You will find other examples on the website.

TEMPLATE

1. **Opinions about Great Issues**
   - The Environment
   - Natural Resources
   - Overpopulation
   - Healthcare
   - Education
   - Leadership
   - Poverty
   - Terrorism
   - Governance
   - Corruption
   - Planned vs. Market Economies
   - Globalization
   - Relativism vs. Absolutism
   - Holistic vs. Myopic Vision
2. **Premises**
3. **Values & Beliefs**
4. **Aspirations**
5. **Personality Survey**
6. **Plan for Further Education**
7. **Career/Avocation Path**
8. **Partnering**
9. **Lifestyle**
10. **Personal Community**
11. **Role in Larger Community**
12. **Financial Plan**
13. **Body Wisdom**
14. **Emotional Wisdom**
15. **Spiritual Wisdom**
16. **Biographical Sketch & Journal**

1. OPINIONS ABOUT GREAT ISSUES

The Environment

The viability of our planet is fundamentally important to our existence. Accordingly, I think it is unwise to risk our well being and that of our children based on the rationale that there might be insufficient proof that we are heading toward trouble. I support those who err on the side of playing it safe, even if it means we may need to simplify our lifestyle. I suspect that those in the future looking back will be astounded by the mindlessness and malfeasance of leaders of various commercial enterprises and government agencies regarding how they dealt with environmental issues. And I suspect those looking back will be astonished by our consumption habits and wonder how we thought we could continue to consume the resources of the planet at such a remarkable rate without deleterious effects. It is becoming increasingly clear that, unless we educate and discipline ourselves regarding our relationship to the environment, we will fail the promise to our progeny and the promise to the rest of those who follow us. Don't we realize that we are contradicting ourselves when we say to our children, on one hand, that we love them, and, on the other hand, we undermine the viability of our planet through selfish, gluttonous lifestyles?

Natural Resources

Unfortunately, due to a lack of vision and moral leadership, we and other peoples find ourselves in an increasingly precarious position when it comes to natural resources. The confluence of environmental degradation, overpopulation, globalization, and over-consumption press the limits of the supply of fossil fuels, water, and food. I believe we would be shaken to our core if we understood the possible outcomes of a lack of coherent and credible strategies regarding such resources. We would be less inclined as individuals to be co-conspirators with those in positions of power who stress narrow self-interests, while ignoring long-term consequences. It is important to understand that too many of us, as mindless consumers and apathetic citizens, have allowed politicians and those who direct commercial enterprises to compromise our future. Unless enough of us reduce consumption and work together in a creative manner to exercise our influence in the governance of natural resources, we should not be surprised by a decline in our standard of living and/or by serious disruptions of social order here and abroad.

Overpopulation

How we deal with the phenomenon of overpopulation will affect the outcome of the challenges we face regarding the environment and natural resources. In their book, *The Population Explosion*, Paul and Anne Ehrlich defined overpopulation as: "When a country's population can't be maintained without rapidly depleting nonrenewable resources (or converting renewable resources into nonrenewable ones) and without degrading the capacity of the environment to support the population. In short, if the long-term carrying capacity of an area is clearly being degraded by its current human occupants, that area is overpopulated." They went on to say: "The United States is overpopulated because it is depleting its soil and water resources and contributing mightily to the destruction of global environmental systems." They added: "Almost all the rich nations are overpopulated because they are rapidly drawing down stocks of resources around the world. They don't live solely on the land in their own nations; they are spending their capital with no thought for the future."

If we accept these observations, how can we ensure that effective leadership will act in the best possible ways? I agree with those who believe that education offers the key to this enormously important and complex problem.

Healthcare

Our healthcare system is broken and out of control. Is it any wonder, given the combination of forces at work within the system.

To capitalize on their interests, insurance and pharmaceutical companies use their enormous power to influence government regulatory agencies and other parts of our healthcare system. At the same time, lobbyists representing medical mal-practice lawyers petition government officials to ensure that the system continues to allow them to sue physicians and hospitals for excessive amounts of money. This increases the cost of insurance and causes the practice of medicine to become so defensive that the quality of care is diminished while the cost of medical services increases. The combination of such self-serving behavior contributes to the shameful facts that a growing number of individuals are uninsured, and that our system of healthcare is underachieving in spite of the enormous amount of resources being applied.

Given this unacceptable state of affairs, I think it is reasonable to assume that those in government and others, who relate to our healthcare system, are guilty of malfeasance and/or incompetence. They should be considered guilty until they prove otherwise by articulating a coherent and moral strategy regarding how to transform the system.

Medical schools play an important role within the system. However, they have been less than progressive due to their myopic dedication to science that honors specialization and conventional modalities of treatment *so absolutely* that it leads practitioners to narrow their focus unduly, and close their minds to new possibilities. It has only been recently that some medical schools, hospitals, and physicians promote integrative strategies of healthcare, even though some of the complementary and alternative modalities they are *now* honoring have been utilized effectively for centuries.

I believe that countless thousands of physicians, nurses, and other practitioners should be commended for their dedication to providing worthwhile healthcare services. However, most remain unaware that they are part of a system that is based largely on industrial-age modeling, where standardized protocols promote the consumption of drugs and the treatment of symptoms and diseases, more than they promote the discovery of causes and the fostering of prevention.

And, we must add to this disquieting equation the fact that most of us do not choose healthy diets and lifestyles. While this reflects our own lack of discipline and common sense, I believe it also reflects the failure of our system of education to teach us systematically and convincingly how to maintain full health. If our system of education did manage to do this and we, in turn, exercised more discipline individually, less healthcare would be needed, and a greater number of us would die of old age rather than costly diseases.

While I believe a market economy functions better than socialism, I do *not* think our healthcare system should function as a set of competitive business enterprises. Healthcare should be considered a cultural institution that satisfies the needs of all citizens. Accordingly, I support a system of universal healthcare that is designed to be self-catalyzing and self-cleansing, rather than a typical government program that is, by design, destined to become highly bureaucratized and inefficient.

Education

The most pivotal institution of modern times, education, is failing its promise, in spite of enormous investments of time and resources. While blessed with many good teachers and administrators, our system of education does not: (1) empower enough of our best and brightest to lead us forward creatively and coherently; (2) enable most of those who follow to differentiate between truth and lies, reality and illusions; and (3) liberate us from insidious prejudices and self-limiting ideologies. As a result, most of us remain confined within a provincial orientation, unaware of our myopia and our underachievement. I do not believe money is the primary cause of this failure, as much as it is conceptual.

We forget that generations ago, while allowing the allure of industrial-age modeling to rule their sensibilities, educators shaped the enterprise of education into a mass-produced commodity. As specialization became the basic organizing technique, educators were driven to put everything in its singular, specific place. The knowledge base was divided with precision into categories and subdivisions, fostering the formation of distinct curricula: Language, Science, Math, Social Studies, etc. This forced teachers to specialize and to function within a top-down, incoherent, self-limiting system of transferring knowledge in schools that, in many cases, function more like factories than learning centers. As a result we have today an insular system, paralyzed by bureaucracy and a lack of vision, which employs curricula so highly fragmented that an objective observer might think there is a conspiracy at work to obfuscate rather than illuminate how the pieces of the puzzles of our existence might fit together. While there is increasing interest in the challenge of integrating the curriculum, there has been little substantive progress. We continue to graduate too many highly-fragmented, overspecialized, disoriented, individuals who are more apt to become submissive cogs in the socio-economic machine of our time, than to function as comprehensively aware, creative participants.

It is with these thoughts in mind that I advance Life Mapping and Social Mapping as empowering, bottom-up processes that enable students to: (1) think more critically and holistically; (2) adapt to increasing complexity, rapid change, and globalization; (3) gain an overall sense of who they are and how they may orchestrate an authentic, satisfying, healthy life; and (4) work with others to build vibrant and sustainable institutions and communities that reflect the heightened awareness of themselves and of the great issues of our time.

Leadership

I believe no amount of speechmaking, religiosity, nostalgia, scientific breakthrough, or orchestration of levers of power will generate a viable future unless the initiative is based on coherent and moral leadership. It is important to remember that, more than anything else, it was a lack of such leadership that determined the decline of all the major cultures that preceded our own.

I appreciate that some would argue that their religion and its leaders provide an adequate guide to a viable future. Adherents claim that if we follow their precepts faithfully, we would fulfill our possibilities. Unfortunately, no major religion has led us forward with a truly *universal* vision that transcends ancient prejudices, self-limiting ideologies, and illusions. Instead, many religions struggle to remain relevant and coherent in the modern world.

In the political arena, it may be difficult to find many leaders who are not tainted by some kind of malfeasance or other serious fault. We seem to have institutionalized mediocrity, as we utilize governance practices that are highly questionable. For example, we may praise our politicians for their skill at compromising to get legislation enacted. However, I suspect we would be highly disheartened, if we understood what principles and long-term interests of ours they violate in the process.

I believe the coherent and moral leadership we need for modern times should be spawned by our schools. They are in the best position to enable our best and brightest students to comprehend our reality holistically and to lead creatively as adults. Unfortunately, as I mentioned in my opinion about education, most of our schools embrace highly fragmented curricula, which encourage overspecialization. They ignore the reality that coherent and moral leadership depends on how *comprehensively* challenges are perceived, rather than on simply having an understanding of the various components of challenges. As a result, we will hear more and more about the inability to "connect the dots," as our leaders struggle to deal with rapid change, increasing complexity, globalization, and the challenge of realizing what is possible and noble for our society.

Poverty

Humankind has the resources and know-how to extinguish poverty. However, we lack the leadership, integrity, selflessness, and corporate structures to get the job done. While we may applaud present efforts, they do not represent a comprehensive, adequately funded, and efficient strategy to deal with the magnitude of the problem, which is exacerbated by bad governance practices and heartless corruption. We are talking about *many millions of people* in Africa and elsewhere who die each year of preventable and treatable causes, including undernourishment, a lack of safe drinking water, malaria, tuberculosis, and AIDS. Even in the United States, the richest, most powerful nation on the planet, profound suffering and/or a shortened life-span are experienced by many people within the lower strata of our society due to poverty.

Somehow, in our egocentric, fragmented, frenzied existence, we feel little shame in having so much to enjoy, while so many human beings suffer and die needlessly. I believe most of us would support, much more generously, programs that work to extinguish poverty within a generation, if there was leadership with vision and determination to design and orchestrate them. Such a goal is within our reach, if we manage our resources and sort out our priorities more judiciously. It is important to realize that sacrificing to help the poor will fulfill us more surely than undue devotion to material wealth and consumption.

Terrorism

The rising tide of terrorism is generating enormous anxiety and fear in many parts of the world. Americans have been caught by surprise. We seem unprepared to fight what could be considered World War III. While the battle lines and enemies are ill defined, the conflict is global and the possible consequences more deadly than any conflict humankind has experienced up to now. While humankind has survived past misadventures resulting from extremism, we should be concerned today because some terrorists and nations, who are violence prone, may soon gain weapons of mass destruction (if they don't already possess them) that can cause the death of tens of millions of people, and make parts of our planet uninhabitable.

I believe that, if the United States is to lead the war against terrorism successfully, we must understand that our great wealth, enormous military power, impressive technologies, and modern lifestyles may hurt more than help us deal with a war of ideas, especially in a world that is rapidly shrinking due to global communications and travel—where highly diverse ideologies and lifestyles are contrasted, and vast economic differences are vividly displayed. Terrorism gains momentum through misunderstanding, hatred, alienation, despair, jealousy, poverty, violence, and through attempts at domination. When we are guilty of hypocrisy and questionable use of power to serve our economic and political interests, it makes it difficult to appeal to the sensibilities of moderates whose political leverage could greatly diminish the energy of the terrorists' campaigns. We must accept that our dubious behavior increases the number of terrorists and strengthens their resolve. Strangely, we have yet to learn that we cannot extol a humanitarian vision and act like a duplicitous, gluttonous bully at the same time.

Governance

Unfortunately, history is not encouraging in terms of showing that humankind has the capacity to govern its institutions in a manner that is effective and sustainable over the long run. Somehow we manage to design and orchestrate them in a fashion that leads, more often than not, to stultifying bureaucracy, wastefulness, arrogance, corruption, and decline. Given this pattern, we should not be surprised by our society's inability to respond effectively to the great issues of our time.

It seems odd to me that we continue to employ traditional, top-down, bureaucratic structures to govern political, economic, and cultural institutions when we know that they will fail their promise sooner or later. Why must we endure such foolishness and remain so vulnerable, given the fact that there are alternative strategies for organizing our institutions?

Most of us would agree that institutions designed to be self-catalyzing and self-cleansing will be more effective and sustainable than constructs that lack these attributes. Nevertheless, these attributes are not employed very often. I suspect this is the case because those who start a new institution or claim to be transforming an established one make sure that they maintain their power and control. Or perhaps, out of ignorance, they simply employ a conventional, top-down, pyramidal model, not knowing its limitations. Unfortunately, once such structures and systems of power and control are in place, it becomes extremely difficult to change them, until a crisis occurs that reveals their weakness.

The alternative to traditional, top-down, bureaucratic structures for governing our institutions is "the learning organizations."[47] Self-catalyzing and self-cleansing, a learning organization understands itself as a dynamic, open-ended system of human beings dedicated to using feedback systems and alignment mechanisms to continually adapt, learn, and grow in order to respond to changes in the environment. The knowledge concerning how to develop learning organizations already exists. We must appreciate the governance principles involved, and demand from our leaders that they utilize them within our institutions or get out of the way.

Corruption

Corruption is more pervasive than we realize. In some countries it is so common that their government is often referred to as a "kleptocracy," that is, "rule by thieves."[55] While in the U.S.A. there is no way of measuring the prevalence of corruption, I suspect that we would puke if we knew the extent of bribery, extortion, cronyism, nepotism, patronage, graft, embezzlement, and other forms of corruption. Like a low-grade infection, it insidiously undermines the health of our institutions and the trust we have in them.

Can we cure this infection? While probably not completely, I believe we can greatly reduce the incidence of corruption, if we recognize that it is we who allow the circumstances to exist within which such misbehavior occurs. If we persevere and work with enough other citizens diligently, we can insist on a re-structuring of our institutions to function organically with checks and balances that keep the levers of power and control out in the open for all to observe and question. We can insist on transparency and accountability with no more backroom deals, no-notice-middle-of-the-night voting, or other malfeasance.

Planned vs. Market Economies

I am more of a capitalist than a socialist. I believe a market economy works better than an economic system in which the means of production are owned and controlled collectively in an effort to effect social equality and an equitable distribution of wealth. However, I believe both ideologies will ultimately fail because they do not fully satisfy the criteria of being self-catalyzing, self-cleansing, and sustainable and because neither prizes equity, justice, and compassion.

Actually, a market economy is self-catalyzing and self-cleansing whenever the dynamics of supply and demand are allowed to function without restraint. However, I do not think it is sustainable, as we know it. Driven mindlessly by power and money, free-market business enterprises affect our political and cultural institutions insidiously to the extent that their long-term viability is undermined. Therefore, it will not matter if our standard of living improves in the short term. Eventually, the "house of cards" will implode.

Unlike Capitalism, Socialism (as we have known it) lacks inherent processes that make it self-catalyzing and self-cleansing. As a result, its institutions are not sustainable in the long term, however good the intentions may be of those who promote its programs. Overall, the reality has been that we have not had the leadership required to create a coherent and moral vision of how the attributes and benefits of a market economy can be *combined* with the value of worthwhile social programs. Such a possibility is within our reach if we incorporate love, compassion, and truthfulness within our institutions. If not, we will become another failed culture eventually, in spite of how rich and powerful we were.

Globalization

Global transportation and communications have been shrinking our planet ever so rapidly. While the pace was relatively slow over the past few centuries, we now are experiencing the rapid movement across borders of capital goods, labor, technologies, and ideas. This convergence generates both positive and negative effects. For businesses it may mean cheap labor and becoming more competitive and profitable. For consumers it may mean lower prices. For others it may mean the loss of a job and a decline in their standard of living.

For those migrating from a poor to a rich country, they may gain employment and access to schools, healthcare, and other public facilities, but at the expense of citizens who are already established in the communities.

Globalization will not stop, given the reality of porous borders and the considerable force of business interests. The challenge was, and continues to be, to comprehend the process of globalization holistically, while appreciating its benefits and responding creatively to its negative effects. In these terms, our federal government has been failing miserably. Presidents and congresses have allowed immigration to get so much out of control that it may now be impossible to generate legislation that is both fair and coherent.

At the core of the chaos we face is the fact that our government, submitting to special-interest groups, ignored its own laws by allowing businesses to employ illegal immigrants without *serious consequences* to those businesses. In spite of our porous borders, we would have had a much more moderate influx of immigrants if jobs were not readily available. And so, while narrow business interests may have been satisfied, we will be living with the consequences of the shameful behavior of our leaders for decades to come.

Relativism vs. Absolutism

Religious absolutism involves unequivocal faith in revelations that underpin one's religion. Assuming that the values embodied in their faith will remain valid forever, followers do not wish to question their belief system and consider the possibility that it may be merely a social construct generated by humans, which can be modified by humans to be more inclusive and more empowering. Therefore, when a religion based on revelation is established as unalterable, it largely precludes reconciling with other points of view and adapting new insights that may materialize during humankind's developmental journey. As a result, religious absolutists may end up supporting convictions long after they have been proven wrong, such as believing that our planet is flat and the center of the universe. A more profound consequence of this kind of closed-mindedness is that some leaders and followers become so extreme in the certainty of their beliefs that they perpetrate destructive crusades and other forms of holy wars in the name of their God. Much of the terrorism we are experiencing today is generated by such absolutism.

On the other hand, relativists believe that the meaning and value of human beliefs and behaviors have no absolute reference. They claim that humans understand and evaluate beliefs and behaviors only in terms of the context of the situation. However, as things stand, relativists find themselves lost in a quandary of unanswerable questions. They do not know what to put in place of belief systems whose premises they deconstructed. Therefore, they have no coherent vision of how to move forward.

If we step back from this turmoil to gain an overview of our dilemma, I think we will find that *both* absolutism and relativism represent dead-ends in the mazeway. Neither illuminates humankind's developmental journey sufficiently. Both embody premises that are fundamentally flawed. Neither will empower social constructs that are self-catalyzing, self-cleansing, and sustainable. I believe, if we learn to accept the possibility of an integral perspective and strive to achieve it, we will begin to transcend the limitations of absolutism and relativism.

In the meantime, growing masses of people, who are overwhelmed by the chaos of our times, retreat fearfully to positions of certainty that religious absolutism offers. I believe this retreat to absolutism will perpetuate, if not amplify, what has been an endless cycle of destruction and despair through the ages.

Holistic vs. Myopic Vision

From premodern to modern to a postmodern worldview, and from absolute to relative truth, humankind's developmental journey has been highly problematic. As history reveals, even the most extraordinary cultures, some of which prevailed for centuries, would not satisfy the fuller test of time. Sooner or later their illusions, prejudices, and self-limiting ideologies would undermine their creative energy, moral authority, and/or relevancy, making them vulnerable to the winds of change and/or to the enemy at their gate.

Today, we find ourselves side by side with competing cultures, each driven by its own brand of illusions, prejudices, and self-limiting ideologies. As individuals within the human drama, you and I find ourselves following the programs of one orientation or another, probably as a result of the accident of the time and place of birth, our family's orientation, and other influences of the socio-cultural setting of our situation, rather than as a result of conscious choice.

Unfortunately, we are not taught to question the premises of our orientation. Instead, we are taught to stay within bounds and remain conceptually imprisoned, unaware of our myopia. We do not realize that what has been an endless cycle of destruction and despair during humankind's history will continue until we transcend ancient prejudices, illusions, and self-limiting ideologies, and, in turn, develop an increasingly holistic vision of how humankind can move forward together creatively, joyfully, and peacefully. Such a transformation of our orientation begins with questions, doubt, and humility, rather than with indifference, certainty, and arrogance; it begins with the perception that most of the great issues of our time are connected, and, unless we connect them coherently and respond constructively, we and our progeny will suffer.

2. PAGE ZERO PREMISES

- As conscious beings made of the stuff of the stars, we are free to shape our destiny. What we become, what we actualize or not, depends on the choices we make; that is, on how well we orchestrate our consciousness to satisfy physical, psychological, and spiritual needs.

- Early humans created language, which enabled them to communicate with one another and to articulate visions of their situation in the mazeway. The stories and the myths that emerged became the basic premises of the programs of the mind that empowered the institutions of the various cultures that ensued. Each set of programs prescribed values and beliefs, and how members of the culture should work together to satisfy their needs.
- As individuals within the ongoing human drama, we find ourselves following one set of programs (worldview) or another, either as a result of conscious choice or by the accident of the time and place of birth, our family's orientation, and other influences of the socio-cultural setting of our situation—religion, schools, government, the media, etc.
- The prescriptions and proscriptions of the programs of the mind we follow are so commanding that most of us are not inclined to question their premises. We simply seek affirmation of what we already believe. Consequently, we allow ourselves to be conceptually imprisoned by illusions, prejudices, and self-limiting ideologies, while ignoring the possibility of adopting a more inclusive and more empowering perspective.
- We are challenged to transcend our myopia and generate an overarching, integral vision of how we can move forward together creatively, joyfully, and peacefully.
- Within an integral perspective we realize that everything is connected and, therefore, everything we do, think, and feel has an effect on everything and everyone else. When we are honest, loving, compassionate, humble, inclusive, and creative we resonate with and add to the coherent patterns of the mazeway. When we are dishonest, hateful, egocentric, arrogant, exclusive, or destructive, we add to the chaos of the mazeway.
- The key to generating a sustainable future is to design institutions that are self-catalyzing and self-cleansing.

3. VALUES & BELIEFS

- I value what is coherent in matter, life, and mind. It is the basis of our existence and of our continuing evolution.
- I value freedom. It allows us to discover our identity and to fulfill our best possibilities, individually and collectively.
- I value knowledge. It helps us become oriented in the mazeway.
- I value creativity. It is an expression of our godlike attributes.
- I value love and compassion. They bind us emotionally and help make us whole.
- I value the family unit. It can be a safe, loving, nurturing environment, and the basic building block of community life.
- I believe it is prudent to doubt, since the search for truth is an asymptotic process; that is, we can get closer and closer, but may never fully reach it. Knowledge is to be questioned not worshiped. Those who claim certainty may open the door to tragedy.
- I believe that science plays a pivotal role in the social process because it helps us expand knowledge and separate truth from illusion.
- I believe that we, as individuals, are the basic unit of the social process, the authentic carrier of reality, not our institutions per se. If not enough of us get our own life together and dare to be great, we should not expect our institutions will.
- I believe we should not rely on top-down prescriptions from institutions and leaders who are overly confident or certain they know what's best for us. Within a coherent, inclusive perspective, the process of fulfilling our possibilities is an organic process—a combination of top-down and bottom-up creativity, generated by leaders and followers who are dedicated to freedom, justice, love, beauty, and the pursuit of truth.
- I believe that we experience serenity and transcend death through the things we create: our ideas, our discoveries, our works of art, our progeny, our example.

4. ASPIRATIONS

- Maintain the capacity to give love and support to my family and to others.
- Ground my life in body, emotional, and spiritual wisdom.
- Explore new ideas and become increasingly creative in a manner that leaves the world a better place.
- Do what I can to further develop and implement The Mazeway Project.
- Continue my quest to gain an integral perspective.
- Live a full life without regrets, and pass away peacefully and gracefully.

5. PERSONALITY SURVEY

There are many personality tests we could take to gain clarity about ourselves. Up to now, I have taken just one of the more popular tests: The Myers-Briggs Type Indicator.

The test revealed that I am what the Myers-Briggs process would refer to as an "INTJ." It represents just one of 16 possibilities that indicate some combination of sensing and intuiting through thinking and feeling on one hand, while, on the other hand, resolving whether one leans toward being introverted or extraverted in a manner that is either judgmental or perceptive.

Those who fall within the INTJ category are described as "having original minds and great drive which they use only for their own purposes. In fields that appeal to them they have a fine power to organize a job and carry it through with or without help. Skeptical, critical, independent, determined, often stubborn, they must learn to yield less important points in order to win the most important. They live their outer life more with thinking, inner more with intuition."

I believe the INTJ category characterizes me better than any of the other 15 categories. The next personality test I will be taking will be the Enneagram.

6. PLAN FOR FURTHER EDUCATION

My education will continue by way of reading and writing, and staying involved in The Mazeway Project. My current reading list includes: *Guns, Germs, and Steel* by Jared Diamon; *Our Endangered Values* by Jimmy Carter; and *American Theocracy* by Kevin Phillips.

7. CAREER/AVOCATION PATH

Having had a long, successful career in business, there is no need for me to resolve another career path. Actually, my involvement in The Mazeway Project has been and continues to be my avocation in retirement.

8. PARTNERING

I have had the good fortune of having two successful marriages. My first marriage ended after three years with the passing of my wife. My second marriage is approaching 38 years. Of course, I learned a lot along the way.

Given how problematic the institution of marriage can be, and how high the divorce rate, it seems obvious to me that more time should be spent exploring the other person's personal profile, especially his or her premises, values, beliefs, aspirations, and lifestyle preferences. The sad fact is that we don't even know our *own* true identity in these terms, let alone know the identity of the other person.

We don't seem to appreciate that the "face" we show to our potential partner may not represent who we may be, even at that moment in time, let alone what we may become as we continue to learn and evolve. It's not a matter that we misrepresent ourselves; it's more a matter of ignorance about our true identity, which we may someday have the good fortune to discover.

Accordingly, this Life Mapping process is beneficial because it helps us learn to know who we are in a systematic manner, and, in turn, it could help us understand the other person.

9. LIFESTYLE

Having become clearer about my true identity, I feel the need to live the rest of my life in a social environment where I can be open and honest in a manner that will help me actualize whatever further possibilities I may have as a sovereign citizen of the mazeway. I do not wish to be a prisoner of the social imperatives of our times, which I believe lead, more often than not, to illusions and to emptiness.

For a person in my situation, the protocols of our culture suggest that I relax, enjoy a worriless retirement that I earned, and progress toward dying as pleasantly as possible. From my point of view, that is *not* my calling.

As things stand, it seems that most people envy the lifestyle my wife and I are experiencing. We have beautiful houses in West Conshohocken, Pennsylvania, and on the island of Nantucket off Massachusetts. And, if that were not enough, we have a condo in the Caribbean on the island of Providenciales in the Turks & Caicos Islands. It is embarrassing sometimes to be referring to how we divide our time among our three places of residence, and, at the same time, we might be mentioning, in a matter of fact fashion, that we will be or have been vacationing elsewhere. While there are many people more resourceful than we, whose standard of living is much grander, I can tell you that it really doesn't matter after a certain point. We have more than we ever dreamed, and need no more material stuff. For me, the fulfillment and the serenity I seek cannot be purchased; it can be found largely in my personal community of family, friends, and associates, as well as meeting the challenges of The Mazeway Project.

10. FINANCIAL PLAN

I placed a high priority on becoming financially independent. It was clear to me early on that, unless I controlled my finances, I could not be free enough to manage the rest of my life on my own terms. While I am among the more fortunate people walking this planet, I hasten to add, it took enormous amount of hard work and discipline.

Regarding a Financial Plan per se, I have one that provides for my wife and me, and, I hope, will benefit our children when we die. My stage in life is much different than that of younger people who should develop a Financial Plan that will help them fulfill their aspirations and lifestyle choices in a manner that is realizable over time.

11. PERSONAL COMMUNITY

I prefer being around people who are passionate about things beyond themselves, rather than self-centered individuals who may already have everything, yet still complain.

I prefer *not* to associate with those who are stuck in routines and resigned to accepting their reality as if there is nothing that can be done about it. In my estimation, we begin to die when we give up and retreat in despair—when that switch goes off inside us, and we are no longer engaged constructively in the social process. We may feel this in retirement more than we do during an active career. I don't think people decide consciously to give up. It seems to be simply a by-product of our life within the socio-economic machine of our times, where its imperatives lead, more often than not, to a psychological black hole that sucks our spirit dry.

I prefer associating with individuals who have somehow managed to become free, open, honest, and creative—those who follow their own sensibilities, rather than mindlessly follow others.

12. ROLE IN THE LARGER COMMUNITY

A combination of activities defines my role in the larger community. Dominating my time and energy is my effort to advance The Mazeway Project. I am also on the Board of

Directors of Resources for Human Development, a member of the Board of Governors of the Greater Philadelphia Philosophy Consortium, and an Associate of the Global Dialogue Institute.

13. BODY WISDOM

My health matters, if I am to participate energetically in the social process, if I am to fulfill my life expectancy, and if I am *not* to become a burden to my family and/or to my community. Accordingly, I believe I should take responsibility for my health in a conscious and constructive manner by accruing Body Wisdom.

The more wisdom I accrue about how to manage my health, the greater the likelihood of living vibrantly. When I do interact with healthcare professionals, I do it more in terms of a participatory process rather than one of submission. I keep in mind that I am the client, and the practitioners are the service providers working for me. Their high-priest status has been granted by my respect for their knowledge and skills. However, I am prepared to question their assumptions and conclusions, since they are not always right.

I have been employing Body Wisdom ever since I learned to deal successfully with an elusive health problem that mystified medical doctors many years ago. I get a medical checkup every year, exercise moderately, and track my diet and weight without being neurotic about it. I take vitamins and minerals, sleep soundly six to seven hours each night, and feel very good.

14. EMOTIONAL WISDOM

It seems to me that I have my emotions under control more than most people. I tend to remain calm under pressure and try to sit back and use the rational side of my being to avoid stressful situations in the first place. When I am confronted with a difficult challenge, I try to respond as constructively as possible without my emotions taking charge. When I experience a major setback, I use my rationality to guide me through the experience, allowing my emotions to inform me, not rule me. At the same time, I try to be compassionate and loving toward others, and empathize with their thoughts and feelings.

15. SPIRITUAL WISDOM

Whatever spiritual wisdom I have comes from the mind of God within me—a gestalt of my mental faculties, the sum of my thoughts, feelings, intuition, imagination, and conscience. An inherent part of the implicate order, it is my ultimate compass, my source of creativity, the means to my liberation and further development.

I access the mind of God within me when I am quiet and peaceful, and motivated by love and selflessness. On the other hand, when I am fearful or selfish, the mind of God remains obscure and inaccessible.

I believe that pursuing spiritual wisdom and seeking an integral perspective represent the same quest.

16. MY BIOGRAPHICAL SKETCH AND JOURNAL

(These final parts of My Life map are presented in the next chapter.)

IX

MY BIOGRAPHICAL SKETCH AND JOURNAL

Having read My Life Map and the other
parts of this book, you know a lot
about me in terms of The Mazeway Project.
Here is the more personal side of my story.

WAY BACK WHEN

Growing up in South Philadelphia was not all that bad. My friends and I mostly hung out on street corners, jostling one another to help resolve who we were and where we stood in the group. With no playground in sight and little to do, we struggled over trivial things as if our lives depended on them. Our view of the world hardly extended beyond the neighborhood and the catechism, while a king-of-the-hill mentality governed our sensibilities.

I cannot attest for the others, but, looking back, I did not like to lose, look stupid, or feel shame. I wanted to fit in, be competitive and respected. This attitude not only pervaded my behavior at play, but in the classroom and at home as well.

At school I may have ranked above average, probably more because I was curious and asked a lot of questions than because I was inherently smarter. Always thinking and pressing the limits of my common sense, I seemed driven more than most to solve the puzzle at hand and avoid being disadvantaged in some way.

Through my first nine years of parochial school, our home life was dominated by my parents' portrait photography business. Determined to succeed, they worked long hours. In spite of how busy they were, I never felt unloved or neglected.

At the end of World War II my parents sold the photography business and moved to Atlantic City where we had vacationed. I finished my secondary education at Holy Spirit High School after struggling to adjust to the new situation during my sophomore year. While many of my classmates and teachers there were wonderful, what I remember more clearly than anything else about high school was how much it hurt to lose the battle for the love of Lillian, a beautiful blond cheerleader with dimples. Otherwise, no remarkable things happened to me until I went off to college. I was a late bloomer.

COLLEGE

In 1949, I began my freshman year at what was then called Drexel Institute of Technology. I majored in Business Administration.

It was difficult for me to adjust and, for the first time, I failed courses. I could not understand why I could excel in math, science, and grammar while literature and history seemed so mysterious and obscure. I not only failed freshman English and History, I received the lowest grades of all in those classes. I was put on probation and needed to attend summer school to keep up.

Failing hurt deeply. At the same time I felt like an outsider because I could not understand the social maze of fraternities. Holy Spirit High had no comparable clubs or organizations to prepare me, while most of the other freshmen at Drexel seemed to fit in effortlessly. The guys in fraternities were having the most fun. I felt diminished.

For the first time in my life, I was confronted with a challenge I might not be able to deal with successfully. Common sense and critical thinking would only take me so far. And, because I was the first in my extended family to attend college, I did not feel anyone at home could help me. This was my problem alone since, at that time, I was not inclined to seek help elsewhere. I don't know if it was shyness, immaturity, or the result of my orientation within parochial schools, where there had been very little dialogue with teachers outside the classroom.

Back then there was no way for me to know about the nature of my learning difficulty. Did I simply lack a particular aptitude? While I felt confused and intimidated, I knew, at some level of consciousness, I was clever enough and persistent enough to adapt. I would have to work harder than others. I would need to decipher the code that obscured the information and recompose it in a manner that made sense to me.

I struggled through my first two years at Drexel, seldom feeling good about myself. At that time, the Korean War was running into its second year. On a whim I decided to join the U.S. Marine Corps. I suppose I did this because I wanted to feel in control of some aspect of my life. Isn't it peculiar what young people leave so readily to fate.

A MARINE

Discipline was harsh during boot-camp training on Parris Island, South Carolina. Two of the three drill instructors had recently gotten back from the front lines in Korea. We came to understand that the reason for their nastiness, at least in part, was their intent on not letting anyone survive camp who they thought would "fink out" in a tight situation on the battlefield.

You may already know a lot about what goes on in boot camp by way of movies you have seen or stories you have heard from those who experienced it. I will not add much except to say that it was a demanding experience for me and useful to the extent that *I firmly resolved that I would do everything in my power never to be so completely under the control of others again.*

I was proud to get through those 77 days in boot camp and to put on my Marine uniform with a private's stripe and the expert medal I had earned on the rifle range. Most of my platoon ended up in infantry training to prepare for Korea. Some did not survive the war. I had the good fortune to be assigned to a Marine Corsair Squadron on the aircraft carrier *Coral Sea*. We cruised the Caribbean and the Mediterranean while training Marine and Navy pilots for the bloody struggle raging on the other side of the world.

Like many youngsters, I had dreamed of becoming a fighter pilot. So, on the aircraft carrier, I felt close to where I wanted to be, despite the fact I was merely an enlisted man fixing electronic gear. I was impressed by those courageous pilots being catapulted into the air in the middle of the ocean and, then, after completing their training mission, found their way back to our ship to deal with the tenuous process of landing on a moving bobbing flight deck—incredibly, even at night.

I was happy with what I was doing. The war was too far off to worry about. It amazed me when I became a Sergeant 13 months after I joined the Corps. These were good times for me and things were about to get better. I had applied for Navy Flight School and couldn't keep the smile off my face when I was accepted. We were anchored off Nice, France, at the time. What a glorious place; I hated to leave it behind. The long, circuitous trip to Pensacola, Florida, was uneventful. A couple of hours after I reported, I was released from the Marine Corps and, in the next breath, became a Naval Cadet.

FLIGHT SCHOOL

It was hard to believe I was actually at Pensacola Naval Air Station, and my aspiration to become a fighter pilot was coming true. I felt lucky and very proud. I knew there were a great many other individuals who would like to trade places with me.

As you would expect, flight school attracts some of the best, brightest, and most physically fit young Americans. In my class, almost all were college graduates; some had advanced degrees. While I had only completed two years of college, I somehow managed to rank seventh in Pre-Flight School out of a class of forty-three. Passionate about what I was doing, it was relatively easy for me to learn about navigation, meteorology, and the mechanical aspects of an airplane. Everything seemed so logical, orderly, and purposeful.

I had none of the feelings of inferiority I had experienced at Drexel, or the belittlement I suffered in boot camp. While there was discipline, Naval Cadets were treated with respect, not only while on base, but wherever we went. The government was investing a lot of money in our training. We felt needed, especially since there was a serious war raging in Korea.

I learned to fly without much difficulty. It was fun, although there were some scary moments. One little experience will always remain clear in my mind. I was just getting used to flying alone, so I was not doing anything fancy—just a young man enjoying the ultimate toy on a beautiful day over the coastline of the Gulf of Mexico. Suddenly, I found myself in a dense cloud, as if someone had put it in my path while I wasn't looking. I had not yet learned to fly via instruments, so I immediately became frightened. The horizon disappeared from view.

The horizon is the fundamental reference point for pilots. It keeps them oriented up there when not on instruments. Without the horizon you can't tell whether you are gaining or losing altitude, flying at an angle, etc. There were instruments staring back at me that I basically understood. They could help if I just stayed calm, but, I was so new at the game, my fear took over. Instinctively I knew I should do little or nothing. The cloud mass could not be that big because, just seconds ago, I was in the clear. Sure enough I was quickly out of the cloud and my friend, the horizon, reappeared. That was absolutely the scariest moment of my life. *I did not like being disoriented and vulnerable. Clearly, I prefer being in control—leaving as little as possible to chance.*

After completing 13 of 18 months of the program, while learning Formation Flying, the war ended. I did some soul-searching, and decided to resign from flight school and return to the challenge of completing my education. While my dream of becoming a fighter pilot would not be realized, I had experienced enough to know I could have done it. To me it was not worth spending another three years in the service, which would have been required if I had gotten my wings. With the country at peace I did not feel obligated, and I learned that the military is not a place for someone like me who values his freedom and independence. As it was, I had become more mature and looked forward to my future confidently. Dealing with course work and the prospect of fraternity life at Drexel did not seem so formidable. I sensed I could navigate my way through the maze of variables that would come my way as my life unfolded. My time in the service had been well spent.

SECOND ROUND AT DREXEL

I returned to Drexel's five-year program. I had three years to go.

The fraternity members I had envied three years earlier were Theta Chis. I simply walked up to their frat house, knocked on the door, and asked if I could board there as a "house freshman." I deciphered that this was the most direct route to becoming a brother. I would be living with them. They could evaluate me directly. If I measured up, I would become a member after going through the initiation process.

As things turned out, I took my role as a brother more seriously than most. I don't think the other members had experienced the loneliness of being on the outside and desperately wanting to participate in fraternity life, as I had during my earlier years at Drexel. I now felt accepted and a part of the mainstream of campus life. This was important to me. It provided an identity. I had one as a Marine and as a Naval Cadet. Now I had an identity as a Theta Chi.

I was proud to have become Treasurer of the chapter within one year. And then what shocked me beyond words was being nominated for president my senior year. It could not be true. I never saw myself in such a role, nor did I seek it.

When told I had won the election, I felt frightened and inadequate, and, at the same time, proud to become president of the most popular and largest fraternity on campus. I was informed that my speech was more inspiring than my opponent's, and the fraternity brothers could identify with my aspirations, even if they were a bit idealistic. I remember working long and hard on my presentation. I did not want to make a fool of myself while telling them what I thought. To me the election process was not political; it was about being completely honest and humble while pressing one's imagination about what was possible.

Schoolwork went much better than during my previous tour at Drexel. And, as a result of my active role in fraternity life, my social life became much more vital. I would never again experience those feelings of inadequacy that plagued me during my "first round" there. And now, as I look back, I realize more fully how valuable it was to me to be part of Drexel's Co-op Program. During the last three years there, I attended school for six months and worked for six months in jobs Drexel secured for Co-op Students. Those jobs were a great value to me, since they provided significant experience in the real world of business and industry.

Upon graduation from Drexel, I was expected to capitalize on my degree in Business Administration and get a job like everyone else. Instead, I loaded my belongings into a new 1957 Dodge sedan, proudly given to me by my parents, and took off for Los Angeles. Unlike my classmates, I journeyed into the sunset without a job and without a plan.

I did not fully know what prompted me to stray from the herd. Perhaps, at some level of consciousness, I thought that doing what was expected of me would have been too easy and predictable. I needed time and space to think. I was free and independent and confident. I knew my life could be shaped any number of ways. I wanted it to be based on my own thoughts and feelings, rather than what was expected of me. I would be upset with myself if, upon looking back on my life, I had readily submitted to the styles of the current social milieu without questioning them—especially since I sensed there was something fundamentally wrong with the ethos of our time.

INTO THE SUNSET

The trip to California was long and lonely. Back then, except for the Pennsylvania Turnpike, there were no super highways along the way. This made the trip much more time-consuming and demanding than it would be today. I traveled on infamous Route 66 more than any other road. I had not realized the USA was so big, beautiful, and diverse. I was especially surprised by my reaction to the Grand Canyon. Its grandeur brought tears to my eyes and amplified my feeling of loneliness. I had spent five long days on the road without having talked to anyone except gas-station attendants and waitresses. I wished I had someone with whom I could share my musing about my life and how it would ensue further west, beyond the canyon. That's when I invented my companion, Azza. From another world within me, she would be all knowing and truthful—a free spirit who would help guide me through the maze of my life's journey.

I asked Azza what she thought of my adventure. "Do you think I'm going off the deep end?"

"No, Tony. I think it's terrific that you elected to escape the pressure to conform."

"Why am I driven to be free? It's not like I know where I'm going, necessarily. I seem to need to make certain it's my life I am experiencing, rather than one directed by others. Do you think I'm being foolish or egocentric?"

"Of course not, Tony. Your adventure is exactly what most people would pursue if they had the courage. Your instincts are valid. Honor them."

I arrived in LA early one June morning in 1957 after driving during the night from Las Vegas. I stopped at a place to get breakfast—one of those drive-in restaurants where they serve you on a tray attached to your car door. I remember going inside to buy a newspaper so I could check the classifieds for a place to live.

As I was walking back to my car to have breakfast, someone tooted a horn at me. It was a good-looking woman in a Cadillac convertible with the top down, beckoning me to her. As if a pulp-fiction writer were shaping the script, my first encounter in LA was to be a young man's fantasy. Believe it or not, the first words from her mouth were, "Are you looking for a place to stay?"

Caught off guard, but being the cool dude I thought I was, I replied, "As a matter of fact, I am." This had to be a dream or an effect of the drive through the desert at night.

She had guessed correctly that, between having New Jersey auto plates, a car full of stuff, and a newspaper under my arm, I needed lodging. She explained, after introducing herself as Louise Mulhern: "I live in a small cottage, which is part of a larger property in Encino. I prefer not to live alone."

I was speechless, so she went on, "I work for a pharmaceutical company. I'm on my way to Santa Barbara on business. You are welcome to visit with the owners of the property, the Harringtons. They live in the big house. If they approve of you and you like the place, you are welcome to move in."

I commented as nonchalantly as I could that it sounded good to me and I would check it out. She gave me her address, and before I knew which side was up, she was gone. It all took place in minutes, like a dream. Was this characteristic of California, or was it simply one of those unusual "accidents" of timing and mutual need that could take place anywhere? I remember feeling excited, yet puzzled, by how direct she was. Keep in mind this was 1957. The wild '60s were not imagined, and I was still growing up, in spite of my time in the military.

Traveling the tangle of LA highways was baffling, even back then. I finally found Encino and the home of the Harringtons. Retired, gray-haired, refined, they showed me the cottage situated behind their dwelling. It was a well-furnished one-bedroom cottage. It was clear what the living arrangements would be. The Harringtons served tea and we chatted. Not too much time had gone by when they said it was all right with them for me to move in. I found myself saying I would return within a couple of days to move in, after taking care of a couple of things. Clearly, I needed time to think about the situation. I knew it could be one of those pivotal decisions.

I found a place to stay I could rent by the day. I read the help-wanted ads; interviewed with a public accounting firm in downtown LA; was offered a job as a junior accountant;

accepted and agreed to start that coming Monday. Things were happening fast. It was time to decide what to do about Louise and the cottage.

I asked Azza what she thought of the situation. "Should I throw caution to the wind and do what most men would do?"

"Only you can answer that, Tony. There's no right or wrong answer in this situation. It is your life to use as you wish."

"Of course, you know my body is saying yes!"

"What about your mind? What's it saying?"

"That's a different story. My mind is going around and around trying to sort out the positives and negatives."

"And your intuition, what's it suggesting?"

"My intuition has generated a blinking yellow light. It is telling me to be cautious."

"Clearly, Tony, you don't need me to answer your question. Your mind and heart are functioning pretty well. I think you already know what's best for you."

When I tell the story of this adventure to friends, the men seem to move to the edge of their chair at this point, eager to hear the story's climax. The reaction of women seems more ambivalent. To me the proposition seemed too perfect, too easy. I felt uncomfortable as I imagined the things that could go wrong. I resolved there was a long future ahead of me to shape. I did not want to have it shaped for me by some problematic situation I could avoid.

I would always honor my intuition.

As it was, I had already proven to myself I could make it to California alone, secure a job, and get situated otherwise. In the process, I realized I had left behind all my friends and family. I was lonely, and it seemed stupid for me to continue my adventure just to assert my independence and to prove whatever it was I was trying to prove. I learned I could do that anywhere. And I would not need to be bothered by the smog.

I called the Harringtons to tell them I had gotten a job in a location not convenient to Encino, and, therefore, I must decline their kind invitation. I believed my lie would be more pleasant for them and Louise to hear than the truth. I called the accounting firm to inform them I had changed my mind and I would not be taking the job. I packed my things and drove north to San Francisco. I decided to take my time traveling the northern route back to New Jersey.

It was late July when I arrived home—almost as if I had never left. But, with all that time I had spent alone, it was as though years had gone by. I felt older and more mature.

MY PARENTS

My parents were responsible for my somewhat charmed life. I can't remember ever having an argument with either of them. Whenever I needed their help, they were always there. My parents helped me out of love, but it was also the faith they had in me to try my best to make something of myself. They knew I was independent-minded, curious, and different. They gave me the time and space to find my way.

My mother, Constance, grew up on a small farm on the Adriatic, east of Rome in the province of Abruzzi. Arriving in this country in 1919 at the age of 11, she remembers how startled she was by the lights of New York City, which she first saw from Ellis Island. Pictures show her as a beautiful young woman only 4 feet 11 inches tall. What they do not reveal was her spirit. She did not know, as she stepped off that boat, how much she would be tested by the challenges she would face.

My father's parents came to this country from Buenos Aires, Argentina, in 1906. Both had migrated to South America from the province of Calabria in southern Italy. My father, Antonio, was born three months after my grandparents arrived in the United States.

My mother and father met through an intermediary and were married when she was 18 and he was 20. My sister Marie was born a year after they were married. My brother Frank followed within two years. I followed him two years later.

Before going into business, my father, in his mid-twenties, worked at Sears Roebuck's main facility in Philadelphia. He and my mother managed to purchase a small row house, one of countless, red-brick, single-family dwellings inhabited primarily by those who worked in the factories, shipyards and other enterprises of the city. Life in America was good for most immigrants who were willing to work hard. Who could have known that in a couple of years the stock market would crash, the banks would fail, the economy would disassemble itself, and my father would become unemployed and so depressed he was unable to work. That combination of events would subject my family to great hardships. With no income to support mortgage payments, the bank foreclosed on our house. Penniless, my family was forced to share a tiny house with my father's sister and her husband in New Jersey.

At twenty-four, my mother remembers holding me in her arms while standing in a government-sponsored bread line with my brother and sister trailing behind her. There were many horrific experiences she endured during those bleak years that framed the rest of her life. Like many depression-era victims, my mother still turns off lights as she leaves a room and walks blocks to save a penny or two. She would do this even if she became the wealthiest person in the world.

As my father slowly emerged from his depression, he became interested in photography. He learned the process, hung out a shingle, and established a portrait photography studio in a small area of my grandfather's house.

The combination of talents and limitations my parents embodied were now at play in the free-market economy, which gradually ascended from its black hole. They progressed one little step at a time until they assembled enough money to buy the storefront house on south Broad Street where I spent most of my early years.

At the end of World War II, after ten years of success, my parents sold the photography business. We moved to Atlantic City where my parents, with their nest egg of money, proceeded to buy and sell Atlantic City real estate as if they were playing the Parker Brothers' game of Monopoly. Over a period of nine years, they owned properties on Virginia Avenue, Park Place, Boardwalk, and Pacific Avenue, as well as in Ventnor and Margate. Among their holdings, at different times, were two boardwalk hotels, an apartment building, and other significant commercial properties. They out-performed many of the local real estate investors as a result of their ability to size-up a run-down property and imagine how they could rejuvenate it. They successfully "pyramided" their assets again and again, looking brilliant in the process. They would have ended up exceedingly rich, if it were not for one serious setback caused by an embezzler, who was their attorney. They had to settle for just being financially independent.

As a youngster I did not pay much attention to my parents' immersion in the world of business. And I don't remember having any aspirations or being encouraged to follow in their footsteps. Somehow—by osmosis, I suppose—I picked up the inclination and the language of an entrepreneur along the way.

ALTERNATIVE FUTURES

When I returned from California, I stayed with my parents in their home near the beach in Ventnor, New Jersey. They never got on my case about my aborted adventure to California. I am sure they wondered what I was going to do next. Their anxiety was relieved when I accepted a position as a junior accountant at Stockton Bates & Company, a public accounting firm in center-city Philadelphia. Tony Parrotto was finally to do what was more or less expected of him.

After six months at the accounting firm, it became clear to me I could do the work and, if I studied very hard, would become a CPA and a more respected, better-paid member of the community. That was not to be.

I met with John Ricketts, the Managing Partner of the firm, to tell him I was resigning to write a book. He was both disappointed and mystified. "Tony, why not write the book and work at the same time?"

It was a reasonable suggestion, but I explained that my nature and limitations were such I could only do one thing well at a time. I did not add that it had become clear to me I would not enjoy a career in accounting.

What was driving my story, at least in terms of career, was that I felt I had the sensibilities of an entrepreneur. One does not go around saying that, but intuitively I felt comfortable with the notion. I had learned some things from the experiences my parents had in business, as well as from the jobs I had during my college years through Drexel's Co-op Program.

From work experience, some of us will decipher the code of the business process better than others. Of course no one keeps score, except to the extent that we might be measured, at some point in the future, by how well we responded to the opportunities that came our way. So I had no way of knowing where I stood in these terms at the time. All I knew was that I recognized that a business enterprise constituted a diverse set of parts which need to be orchestrated as a whole system. I believed I could learn, given enough time, the idiosyncrasies of most business enterprises. In addition, I was highly motivated to become an entrepreneur because I believed it would lead me to greater freedom.

It was unclear what I would actually do with the freedom. I suppose it was just a matter of not wanting to be in a position where others were telling me what to do and how to behave. Somehow I was different than others my age—not better, just different. I wasn't sure what it was except that it seemed to me that most of my contemporaries were not as curious or inclined to think critically and imaginatively. They simply accepted the reality of their situation and raised fewer questions. While they went along with the flow of things, I found myself sitting back and quietly observing what was going on, as if it were a grand puzzle I wanted to understand and solve.

What I did not realize at the time was how fear of shame was driving me forward. Evidently, from my experience hanging out on street corners and jostling back and forth with my friends to resolve who we were and where we stood in the group, I came away with a fear of losing or looking stupid. My pride is such that, whatever challenges I would face during my life's journey, I would go out of my way to avoid making mistakes and to succeed. As a result, I am now inclined as an adult to ask questions unrelentingly to find out as much as I can about the challenge at hand before moving forward.

Now, as I look back, I understand why I felt compelled to find one square foot of truth on which to build a coherent view of reality and a credible life. I wanted to know the unvarnished truth about our situation and avoid perspectives based on illusion and self-limiting ideologies. Intuitively, I realized that a faulty perspective would make me vulnerable to appearing ignorant and to not fulfilling my best possibilities. Regarding other people, I wondered where the confidence and certainty that comforted them came from. I wasn't sure whether I should envy or feel sorry for them.

PATH TO FINANCIAL INDEPENDENCE

My effort to become an entrepreneur began in an unusual manner. My father and most of the other men in my family were bald or balding. While not talked about, I assumed they did not like it. With my own hairline showing signs of receding, my vanity compelled me to find out if anything could be done to prevent what seemed to be my fate.

My research revealed that, other than superficial articles in popular magazines and some technical articles in medical journals, there wasn't a coherent explanation for laymen about the nature of this problem and what could be done about it, if anything. It seemed to me there must be hundreds of thousands of other men who were concerned about baldness. Perhaps I could write a book on the subject that would satisfy the wide, if unspoken, demand.

So here I was, at the early stages of modeling a new business, one small enough to be within my range of capabilities. I had envisioned a product for which I deduced there was a demand. Then I developed a marketing strategy that would satisfy that demand. If my assumptions were correct, all I had to do was put it all together and move forward.

I proceeded with the development of the manuscript slowly and meticulously. It took me a while to synthesize the data and fashion a schematic for the book. Fortunately, I was living with my parents and had their support.

Here is a brief outline of what I discovered about the subject.

We know our genetic makeup determines what we will look like as we grow up. It's been less apparent to us that our genes also determine how we will grow old. Baldness, grayness, wrinkling, diminishing vision, degeneration of our muscles and bones, and other characteristics of aging are governed by genes. Accordingly, the data revealed, quite straightforwardly, that male-patterned baldness is not treatable, just as the other characteristics of aging are not treatable. Here was a perfectly reasonable conclusion, one reinforced by one's own direct perception that male-patterned baldness seems to run in families.

Most writers would stop there and simply summarize the data for a magazine article; there was not enough material for a book. In my case, however, I was not content to end the inquiry there. I felt the data were promoting an oversimplified, if logical, conclusion. Something was left out of the equation. A question was haunting me—one that seemed both obvious and important.

I understood the logic of the conclusion that our genes prescribe how we grow old, but my intuition suggested there had to be some variable in the equation not being addressed directly. The question was: Do most of us grow old *prematurely*, and, to what extent, unnecessarily so? That is, do we *not realize* the optimum outcome physically due to variables over which we have control?

This fascinated me and demanded I explore the subject further. It would lead me to the concept of Body Wisdom, which I described earlier.

Now I planned to write two books—one about hair and the other on the subject of Body Wisdom. The combination represented a huge challenge for someone with my background. I struggled with the projects, in fits and starts, over a period of three years—an enormous amount of time by most standards. During that time I was dependent on my parents' generosity and on income derived from several meaningless jobs. That my perseverance was being tested would be an understatement.

I am not entirely sure what compelled me to carry on beyond so many moments of despair. It was certainly not the prospect of becoming a published author. I suspect my primary motive was the prospect of making money to become free and independent. I was not interested in material things as much as wanting to be free to author my life on my terms, and not be, unnecessarily or unwillingly, a subject or a prop in scenarios governed by others. At the same time, I felt driven to achieve a level of coherence and excellence that would at least satisfy my own sensibilities, if not the sensibilities of others. I was also genuinely curious about the subject matter, especially Body Wisdom. I wanted to understand how such knowledge was connected to the rest of our existence. As it was, I could not satisfy these needs without sacrificing a significant amount of time and energy.

Whitmore Publishing Company

With one completed manuscript in hand, I proceeded with my plan to publish and market the book on my own. With the financial help from my parents, I started Whitmore Publishing Company in 1961. I selected the name, Whitmore, because it sounded English and part of the "establishment."

If I had known all that was involved in the publishing process, I might have gone the conventional route and tried to get the book published by an established company. Among many other things, I needed to learn about book production and promotion. I sorted out the vendors in Philadelphia and settled on those who would design, typeset, print, bind, and promote my book.

I must have been unusual. I was very thorough, organized, and passionate about what I was doing. I impressed the vendors enough to receive four job offers. The offers were timely since running a one-book publishing company is not a full-time affair. And I had to start some kind of career, especially if my book did not sell as well as I was hoping.

The most appealing job offer was from Breig Associates, an advertising agency specializing in book publishing accounts. It was located on Walnut Street off Rittenhouse Square in Center-city Philadelphia. From the same offices, Mrs. Breig also managed a small book publishing operation, Dorrance & Company, Inc. I would work for both companies as a utility person until I found a useful niche.

With three other investors, Jean Breig had taken over the ownership of Dorrance & Company from Colonel Gordon Dorrance, who had retired not long before I arrived on the scene. A member of the family that founded the Campbell Soup Company, the Colonel started Dorrance & Company in 1920 as the first subsidy book publisher in the United States and Canada. He established the company to help new and/or unknown authors. His guiding philosophy was that the book-publishing medium should be open to all who have something of value to communicate.

Over the years this segment of the book-publishing business was often referred to as the vanity press—a derogatory characterization. The high priests of the industry—traditional publishers, critics, and bookstore operators—felt they were society's arbiters of what the public should read. If the cost of publication had to be subsidized by the author, they generalized that the book was probably inferior.

Philosophically I agreed with the Colonel. Being sensitive about how arrogant and arbitrary those in authority can be, I knew the debate was a choice between two principles: free access to the public or fearing that some poorly written book would see the light of day.

As it turned out, I found myself spending more time on Dorrance & Company matters than in the advertising agency. At least I already knew something about book production, and the other things involved were easy for me to learn.

Pivotal Decision

At this point my story takes some sudden twists and turns.

A few months into the job, it became clear Dorrance & Company was not doing well. Among other things, there was a cash-flow problem. The three outside investors in the company feared Philadelphia National Bank would call the company's loan for which they were personally responsible.

As I studied the problem, I realized the owners, as well as the company's outside public accountant, misinterpreted one important item on the company's balance sheet. If this perception of mine was correct, Dorrance & Company was more viable than they thought. Furthermore, in spite of my short time there, I knew the company could be managed more effectively, even though it seemed strange to think I might know how. While the others were prepared to retreat, I saw it as an opportunity.

I called my parents and asked them to lend me enough money to pay off the loan. Once I got their promise, I proposed to the owners of Dorrance & Company that I would pay off the loan with the bank if I received in return one-half interest in the company. My offer was accepted immediately and, in a matter of days, I was on my way to becoming an entrepreneur. Jean Breig and I were now the owners and operators of the company.

I applied all my time and energy to the challenge of turning the company around, which I did. After only two years, I owned one-half of the advertising agency as well, in exchange for giving up one-half interest in Whitmore Publishing Company. Concerning corporate titles, I was executive vice president of Breig Associates and of Dorrance & Company, and I was president of Whitmore Publishing Company. Together, these three entities may not have been a big deal, but I was certainly gainfully employed, on a good career track, and happy with what I was doing.

Jean Breig

As things became clear, I realized that I was more an entrepreneur and creative generalist than anything else. I was not an exceptional publisher or advertising person, but I knew enough about those roles to be able to put things together and make systems work. I instinctively knew how to compose maps of where we were and how we should proceed to survive. I not only assembled financial statements which I understood absolutely, but also maps of the marketplace, of the skills our employees needed to embody, as well as office space and equipment. While almost everyone else around me was better educated and seemed smarter, they could not do what I was able to do. The process of effectively directing a whole business would remain obscure to them. To me it was simply a matter of hard work and applying common sense to building maps to direct us forward.

However, I could not have done this without Jean Breig at my side. She was my mentor, my confidante. She validated me and listened to my dreams. She thought I was brilliant and respected my tenacity and willingness to work hard and figure out what to do next.

An accomplished poet, Jean Breig was a graduate of the University of Pennsylvania and president of both the Philadelphia Booksellers' Association and the Philadelphia Book Clinic. She was known, among other reasons, for the national awards she had won for her sensitive handling of the promotion of *The Kinsey Report* for W.B. Saunders. She was married and had a young daughter.

Jean and I spent a lot of time together. We often had lunch at the Philadelphia Art Alliance and the Downtown Club. Through her I met with the heads of the major Philadelphia book publishing companies: J.B. Lippincott Company, W.B. Saunders, Chilton, Fortress Press, Lea & Febiger, as well as the leaders of some other Philadelphia institutions. We would go to New York and have lunch at the Algonquin Hotel, the site of the famous Algonquin Round Table where writers and others in the creative arts would assemble socially to discuss new ideas and gossip.

Doors were open to me because the doors were open to Jean Breig. I was learning more than I realized about the subtleties of manners and other social protocol. It was like going to finishing school, although I knew some rough edges would always remain part of me.

During that time, I lived at 2031 Locust Street near Rittenhouse Square in a beautiful apartment on the eleventh floor overlooking South Philadelphia. Just twenty blocks beyond was the neighborhood where I had roamed as a cute young kid trying to find my way.

While my book did not make me rich, it did sell about 8,500 copies in the United States. My New York agent sold the publishing rights to a British company, which distributed copies in most of the other English-speaking countries of the world. In addition, a major French magazine-publishing company bought the right to use excerpts from my book.

More important was the fact that I felt good about myself—a bachelor at 32, with a beautiful apartment, associating with interesting people, learning about all kinds of things.

However, in spite of the benefits of being under Jean Breig's wing, I felt the need to be on my own—to see how far I could press my limits. What I resolved to do was going to be painful no matter how I proposed it to Jean. I was counting on her to understand. If she did respect me and want the best for me, she would support my intentions. Jean knew I was always honest and loyal to her.

I proposed that I return to her my half-interest in the advertising agency and give her a sum of cash, while I would go away with total ownership in Dorrance & Company and Whitmore Publishing Company. There were tears, but I think she knew, probably long before it had occurred to me, that I needed to be free to shape my life on my own terms. I would always love and be grateful to Jean Breig.

An Entrepreneur

Whitmore was a fledgling one-book company that could not support me. Dorrance & Company became my focus. I filled key positions to compensate for the loss of Jean Breig.

I was learning that being an independent entrepreneur is certainly a test of one's resourcefulness. You are confronted constantly with questions about products and services, clients and employees, equipment and supplies, leases and loans, accounting and taxes, time and energy, technologies and the future. Clearly, dealing with this range of issues requires someone who is more a creative generalist than someone who is skillful in only one or two areas, especially when a business is small.

To succeed, I needed to press my limits and immerse myself in every facet of the business. While I did learn to delegate, I would always remain in touch with enough details of the operation to reinforce my overview. To me, I was either in full control or not at all. While others could make up for my deficiencies with their considerable skills and energy, I supplied the vision and the entrepreneurial thrust, for better or worse.

LOVE

Having allowed my commitment to business affairs to consume my time and energy, I found myself at 33 not dating anyone and feeling very lonely. To make matters worse, there were hardly any females left in my tattered personal phone book who were not married or did not live far away. I would have to figure out how to build a social life from ground zero. I knew the first step was to open my mind and heart.

I thought of Mary Lou Wilkenson, whom I would see from time to time at Sunday Mass. She also lived in center-city Philadelphia. When I called her, she invited me over to join her and a friend for coffee. That's when I met Virginia Sullivan. While nothing exceptional happened during that get-together, I knew I wanted to see Ginny again.

A week later I got up the courage to call her. We went out to dinner and got along very well. It was September, 1964.

We continued dating; met each other's family and friends; fell in love; and, by the time Christmas arrived, we were engaged to be married. I did not need any more time to know I wanted to spend the rest of my life with her. I believed Ginny felt the same way about me. Everyone was happy for us.

Ginny was from a large Irish-Catholic family in Lansdowne, Pennsylvania. I still remember being overpowered by the other family members' boisterous behavior at Sunday dinners. Her mother, Katherine, presided, while her children, grandchildren, and friends bellowed their points of view and showed their zest for life. I was very quiet and must have been perceived as a poor fit into their family. Ginny was also the quiet, sensitive one in her family, as I had always been in mine.

Ginny, 29 at the time, was a graduate of Rosemont College and a probation officer for the County of Philadelphia. West Philadelphia was her beat. Most of her parolees were black. It was painful to hear her stories about their struggle. Ginny wanted to help them as much as she could. She realized she had been advantaged: Her father had been a successful physician, making it possible for her family to enjoy the good life in the suburbs.

On April 24, 1965, eight months from the time we met, Ginny and I were married at Saint Philomena's Church in Lansdowne. After a great wedding ceremony, a cheerful reception for some 200 relatives and friends, and a couple of plane rides the next day, we enjoyed the first week of our honeymoon in Old San Juan. The second week was spent at Little Dix Bay on Virgin Gorda.

We loved one another and shared our dreams of making the world a better place, each in our own way. I can't recall ever quarreling with Ginny. While each of us could be quiet and moody, we tried to be sensitive about one another's needs.

We soon became a traditional family and were captured by its imperatives. Our first daughter, Katherine (K.C.), was born nine months after our marriage. And, Virginia (Gina) was born just 19 months later. We lived in a restored row house on Brandywine Street near the Art Museum. While the homes there were modest, it was considered an up-and-coming neighborhood.

Dorrance & Company was located a few blocks away. Its proximity accommodated my long hours at work. I was still plugging away, making sure we would always be secure. While Ginny and I had gotten a late start, we were now a beautiful young family.

The time was the late winter and early spring of 1968. The country was in turmoil. The evening news was dominated by the Vietnam War and the various protest movements. Martin Luther King was making history. Robert Kennedy was campaigning to be nominated for the presidency. The Beatles' music dominated the airwaves.

While the world seemed to be in a state of disarray, Ginny and I had a lot to be thankful for. We had a neat house in a friendly neighborhood, loving families, good friends, and my business was progressing well. Our only concern was our daughter, K.C. Besides *not* talking; she was acting strangely. Evidently, our friends and relatives had recognized and accepted the likelihood that something was wrong before we did. Through our pediatrician, we scheduled an appointment with a neurologist at Children's Hospital for April 24; I will not forget the date because it was also our third wedding anniversary.

Little did we know that, over the next few months, our family's existence would be turned upside down, inside out, and ripped apart at its core.

Tears come now because of what I need to tell you to make my story whole.

SORROW

Ginny always allowed me to do my thing and focus on my business and my dreams. On this fateful day, she was experiencing pain as a result of the gallbladder operation she had had five weeks before. She was scheduled to see her surgeon sometime during the next week, but decided to see him that day instead, April 17. My mother was babysitting. I was in a class at one of IBM's training facilities in Bala Cynwyd.

I remember taking a walk after lunch on that bright sunny day. I had time to waste before the next session began. From a patch of grass near Lord & Taylor Department Store, I picked up a wild flower and put it in the buttonhole of my lapel. It was unusual for me to relax and reflect. At that moment life was good!

Later in the afternoon, upon arriving back at my office, I received a telephone call from the surgeon's office at Jefferson Medical Center. As if rehearsed, the nurse stated, "Something has happened to your wife. Please come over as soon as possible."

My father happened to be in my office at the time I took the call. Before I said a word, he knew something bad had happened.

The fifteen-minute drive to the hospital was a surreal experience. I did not know I was already in shock from the products of my imagination, which was informing me about all the horrible possibilities. It was pure agony not knowing. At each traffic light, people seemed to be walking in slow-motion. I realized later my body and senses were being distorted by the terror of the moment.

I don't recall where or how I parked my car outside the busy hospital. All I remember is, when the elevator door opened on some upper floor, two physicians in white coats were waiting for me. It had to be a dream or some altered state of consciousness. This could not be happening. It was too preposterous, staged too perfectly. But it *was* real.

My wife had died. This meeting was painful for the surgeon who had performed the procedure and for our family doctor who had recommended him. I tried to remain calm as they explained how it happened. My legs wobbled. I had to sit down. They gave me some pills which I held tightly in my hand but did not take. The doctors seemed greatly upset. I remember feeling sorry for them. They chose their words carefully. My mind and heart raced for cover. I knew whatever they said and whatever questions I asked would do nothing to change the stark reality of the situation.

An emotional force wanted to take me down, but, through the bleakness of the moment, I knew I had to survive. K.C. and Gina were going to need me more than ever. And there were my parents, other family members, friends, and the gang back at the office who needed to know I would get through this ordeal. My heart was ripped, but my mind seemed clear.

My mother was angry at Ginny for not returning home that day when she promised. She was unaware of the news she and my father would hear when I returned. I can't think of anything I have done in my life more difficult than telling them Ginny was dead.

When I arrived home, I could not speak. I simply could not utter the words, but my body language and tears were telling my parents something terrible had happened. That minute or so of silence seemed like an hour as they agonized over my deep distress, not knowing its exact cause. The words were finally spoken haltingly, as I told them what I could. They were the most painful moments of all. The actual telling of what happened somehow made it more real and final.

Ginny had complained to the doctor she was experiencing pain as a result of her gall-bladder operation. The surgeon explained to me that he decided to give her two injections of

Xylocaine. As he was completing the first injection, she went into deep shock. He could not rescue her.

During such times, most of us realize life is tenuous and that we take too much for granted. I felt guilty I had not spent more time and energy with Ginny and the children. Philosophically I had long accepted death as part of life's equation, but I was not prepared for the demise of someone so close to me and so young. A bright, personable, lovable woman of 33 was taken out by what may have been a mistake by a surgeon at a well-known medical institution.

The funeral proceedings remain a blur of pain and emotions. I do recall a long conversation I had with Tom McKenna, a close friend of the Sullivan family who was an English teacher at Malvern Prep. I sensed he was assigned to keep me busy while the long procession of mourners viewed Ginny for the last time. It was then I realized it is the love of family and friends that are so important to get us through difficult times. Without such support, we could easily retreat into a deep depression in our pressing need to escape the pain.

I remember not wanting to focus on all the things that could have been—what I call the what-ifs. If only I had gone to the doctor's office with Ginny, perhaps I would have discouraged her from getting the fatal injection. Did she not tell me she was going to the doctor to spare me from any concern? Did she submit to the injection because she wanted to eliminate her postoperative pain so she could cope with the children and be more pleasant around me? If only I were not preoccupied with my business, I would have been accessible to her and more aware of her difficulties. Many what-ifs pervaded my senses. I wanted them to go away.

With Tom I sought out something in my reality to talk about that would comfort me. I found myself articulating my interest in education and how the curriculum could be integrated. He was a high school English teacher so I felt he would understand. I remember expressing my thoughts and feelings in an intense passionate manner in what must have seemed to Tom to be an effort to mask my distress. He may not have paid much attention to my rambling, especially since he was upset, too. He had known Ginny much longer. I was not the only one suffering.

That incidental conversation was highly therapeutic for me. It gave me the opportunity to affirm that there was a future for me, in spite of my misfortune. I had a role to play, a mission to accomplish.

There was no way of knowing my interest in unraveling a major puzzle of our existence would motivate me for the rest of my life and carry me through other moments of despair. It would not matter if I did not solve the puzzle. It was simply important to be creatively engaged in a project that pressed my limitations, a project that reached beyond me.

I wondered what Azza thought about all that had happened.

"I know, Tony, how much you are suffering. I wish I had a magic wand that could change your reality. You are being tested, and, so far, you are holding your own. Don't give in to feeling sorry for yourself. There's nothing to gain. Are there any questions you want to ask me?"

"No."

I managed to carry on steadily and without bitterness. I knew many of my relatives and friends were worried about me, and I did not want to add to their burden by going into some deep funk. And they were concerned about my children, even though they were too young to know their mother would never touch them again. And there were Virginia's friends and family who had known her much longer. I will never fully appreciate how sorry they felt for my wife and our children, and for their own loss.

I was to be burdened with another of life's misfortunes just a week after Ginny died. On the date of our third wedding anniversary, I met with the neurologist at Children's Hospital to learn K.C.'s diagnosis: she had brain damage, which probably occurred during the pregnancy or at birth. The prognosis was unclear. We would have to wait and see. Already numb from a sorrowful week, I received more bad news from someone else in a white coat at a hospital. I remember sitting there helpless. Did I make some kind of mistake? Was there something I could have done about it? Was it the fault of the obstetrician who was so cocky about knowing the exact expected date of birth? Did he wait too long before admitting her to the hospital to deal with her toxemia and elevated blood pressure, which in turn led to a quickly scheduled Caesarian-section birth? Why aren't physicians perfect in the role of high priest we bestow upon them and then honor so unquestionably?

THE SUMMER OF 1968

I know the script that follows would be rejected by any teacher or producer for being too preposterous. This could not have really happened. Who was writing the script? Is there such a thing as divine intervention? Or does good fortune result from sorting out our mind and heart to help us find our way?

The plan was for my parents to take care of the children, while I went through the process of "regrouping." My mother-in-law, Katherine Sullivan, suggested we hire one particular babysitter Ginny was very fond of to help my parents at their home in Ventnor.

The babysitter, Linda Sue Peacock, was just finishing her junior year at Temple University. I really did not know her very well; Ginny was the one who had interacted with her most of the time.

I interviewed Linda, and we agreed she would work with my parents in Ventnor for the summer. I was to visit on weekends or whenever I was able to get there.

As the events unfolded, I spent a lot of time with Linda and the kids—on the beach, during walks and at meals. One early July evening, I invited her to come with me to see a rerun of *Gone With The Wind*. It was not a date—just a platonic pairing so I would not have to go alone. Our outing was innocent enough. Linda was in a serious relationship with a pre-med student to whom I had been introduced. And I was a widower in mourning.

It did seem strange to be sitting next to her during that long movie—nice not to be by myself. Of course I could not tell what she was thinking or feeling. I knew she was not spared pain from the tragedy. Evidently, she and Ginny had gotten along very well. Linda was shocked when she called my house the day after Ginny died; she was unaware what had happened. Evidently, my mother answered the phone and had to explain the situation. It was a sad exchange. And now, three months later, she was out with me and involved in a drama that was being scripted by the rush of our emotions.

I had already become very fond of Linda. It went beyond feeling gratified that my children were being cared for by such a warm, sensitive, and personable young lady. I enjoyed being around her, and I sensed she liked me. Whether it was fate or our wills at work, we were allowed to get to know one another, innocently, within a safe cocoon granted by the tragedy we shared.

But I was a thirty-six-year-old widower with two babies, whose mother had died just three months before. Linda was still in college at twenty-two and practically engaged. While these two profiles were incompatible, the fantasy of the possibilities carried me forward, masking some of the persistent pain. It felt good to dream, but I knew it could not come true.

Our movie date was uneventful, other than putting our own musings into play. I went back to Philadelphia and Linda continued her job as a mother's helper.

AGONY

While my heart was revealing how I felt, I wanted to rely on my mind and its intuition to guide me. I had seen too many undesirable outcomes resulting from emotions driving decisions.

But this would not be a time I listened to reason. My emotions would prevail as a confluence of events pressed Linda Sue Peacock into my life. I was falling in love.

I do not know if I will ever be able to fully explain what I was experiencing. I imagined the others involved in the tragedy were slowly working through their grief. However, my emotions were probably traveling many times faster. I lived and relived the tragic event countless times, suffering again and again, which in some strange way warped time for me. While it may have been just three months, my torn heart had had enough, and simply wanted to try to become whole again. At the same time, I realized grief could not simply be willed away; it would haunt me every conscious moment until, I suppose, it was done with me—which could be forever.

Each day seemed endless as my mind and heart struggled to reconcile their differences. The social pressure was subtle. I could feel it although no one uttered a single critical word to me directly. It was as if I were an untouchable, the wounded one whose emotional life hung precariously in the balance. The sum of my thoughts and feelings pressed me to begin rebuilding my life. I resolved I could be the sorrowful widower and Linda's suitor at the same time. There would be no way of knowing if I were fooling myself. No one could prescribe when and how to build such an equation, and I believed it would be unfair for others to judge me. It was my life. I felt there was only one person who could sway me from the course I seemed driven to pursue: Mrs. Sullivan, Ginny's mother. It would only be for her that I would hesitate.

And so, my heart leaped forward with abandon, wanting our platonic dance to continue. I was hoping Linda would transcend all the good reasons that stood in the way of taking our relationship further.

In my mind, however, the debate continued. Loudly and clearly, it told me the situation was being catalyzed by my highly emotional state, which made me vulnerable to behaving foolishly and subjecting myself and others to embarrassment. I tried to maintain conventional standards and keep a safe distance for everyone's benefit, as well as my own emotional survival. But that rational insight did not stand. Our dance continued.

As the gods would have it, Linda and I found ourselves drawn together closer and closer, as we shared our thoughts and feelings. We glided forward like two youngsters tantalizing one another with an endless series of what-ifs. The music was more intense, and our dance through the minefield of emotions became more complex, while only a kiss was needed to satisfy our bond. I could not tell if I was simply grasping to fill the void to survive my anguish, nor could I discern what torment Linda may have been experiencing that she did not share with me. To me it felt like a teenage romance and my emotional life had been recharged by the suffering. At the same time, fear hung over us because we knew our newfound bliss could be shattered by one mistake or the cruelty of social pressure.

How does someone as young as Linda deal with such a rarefied situation? How does this sorrowful older man know what's right?

As it turned out, I was the one who made the mistake that smashed our moment of joy.

I had not mentioned the emerging relationship between Linda and me to anyone else. I assumed my parents were bewildered by the fondness we were displaying for each other, but chose to remain silent.

After dinner one evening in late July, we were just sitting around chatting, while K.C. and Gina were crawling around. Was this the new family combination about which I had dreamed?

The doorbell rang. Linda's boyfriend had arrived. It was not the first time he was at our house. But it was the first time he was there when I was there, since I fell in love. Somehow, I had displaced Ed from the equation. Evidently, Linda had not. Everyone else seemed so casual as Ed settled in, reinforcing his relationship with Linda in my presence. I tried to remain calm but escalating emotions were spinning me out of control.

I wondered why Linda did not get Ed out of there, somehow, to protect my aching heart. She had to know how I felt, but she seemed unaware of my dilemma. When I could not take the pain any longer, I pulled Linda aside and told her to ask Ed to leave. She did.

By the time I arrived back home in Philadelphia, my emotions were out of control; I was not interested in trying to be rational. I got my mother on the phone and told her I was going to tell Linda to pack her bags and leave the house the next day—she could no longer be the mother's helper. Linda was put on the phone and I told her directly she was dismissed because of her insensitivity. She was shocked and did not know what to say, but accepted my demand without a challenge.

Alone is an absolute term. If you are not with anyone else, you are alone. How does one describe a compounding of being alone? And how do we survive such desperate moments when our world is shattered beyond repair? In our despair we are not sure whether we are responsible for our dilemma or whether fate had resolved that we must suffer further. I only had Azza to comfort me.

"Tony, Tony, What can I say? You have managed to back yourself into a pretty dark corner."

"I can't remember ever behaving so irrationally. I guess I'm more fragile than I thought. I wish I could replay that last scene."

"What would you do differently?"

"While it's been a long two weeks of desolation, I have been able to restore my equanimity somewhat and reflect on my behavior. I thought through the sequence of events that led to my mistake. Most people might excuse me. Nevertheless, it was a serious mistake."

"What are you referring to, Tony?"

"I had been compelled to drive my relationship with Linda to a successful union at breakneck speed, desperate to fill my life's voids. What's clear to me now is that Linda was driving forward more slowly, trying to sort out what was best for the long life ahead of her. Perhaps we were both going in the same direction, but she was at a different place in the evolution of our relationship."

"Where does that leave you?"

"What I am uncertain about is whether Linda had actually intended to take Ed out of the equation. If I had kept my cool and allowed her time, maybe our relationship would have developed further."

"Do you think you will ever find out what could have been?"

"I don't know, but I intend to try. Wish me luck."

Highly anxious, I picked up the phone and called Linda's apartment. Her roommate answered the call. I left a cryptic message for Linda to call me. I did not move from my chair as I waited in agony for fate to play its next card.

I sat there feeling sorry for myself, not knowing whether I wanted time to move forward quickly or not. Since I feared the worst, the time spent fantasying about the best possible outcome was comforting. I had always thought I was highly rational and had my emotions under control, but I was now a different person. Things would never be the same. The events of my life would forever be framed by Ginny's sudden death.

The phone rang. I paused a moment, not to seem too anxious, and to extend my fantasy there could still be a future with Linda. Who is writing this script? Please tell me what to say.

Linda stated she was returning my call. The tone in her voice was pleasant, as if firing her two weeks earlier had not happened.

I asked how she was doing. The light-hearted trivial exchange that followed seemed to be an effort on her part and mine to avoid any comment that would end the conversation. Expressing itself between our lines was the hint that reconciliation was possible. This encouraged me to ask if I could come over to chat. When she said yes, I tried not to reveal how ecstatic I was.

We went out for coffee and talked for a long time, rebuilding the bridge between us. I could hear the music playing again. Our dance would continue.

She came back with me to my house. She never left. That was 37 years ago.

ECSTASY

Linda Sue Peacock and Anthony J. Parrotto. A peacock and a parrot—what a beautiful combination!

On August 31 we were married by a priest in a quiet ceremony at St. James Roman Catholic Church in Ventnor. Only relatives and close friends were invited to the ceremony and a small reception in Atlantic City. A range of emotions between joy and grief pervaded the moment. I wish I were a poet to be able to describe them. It was a special time.

Of course we did not know the gods were with us. No doubt our parents were praying for us, even though they were certain, and everyone else seemed certain, the marriage would not last. Only four and one-half months of time had passed since Ginny's death. Linda and I transcended social protocol, not out of defiance, but out of confidence that our minds and hearts would not fail us. We knew it would be good for us, and, as a consequence, good for the children. At that time, no one could comprehend how such an unusual sequence of events and impulsive behavior could lead to a relationship that would continue forever.

The rip in my heart caused by Ginny's death has not completely healed. Still tender to the touch, little things bring back tears easily.

LINDA AND K.C.

Our children were to stay with my parents in Ventnor through Linda's senior year at Temple. We spent our weekends there. Those nine months allowed time for Linda to go through the difficult transition between finishing her life as a student and beginning her new role as a stepmother to two young children. It also granted Linda and me time to quietly shape the beginning of our life together.

The greatest challenge my parents, Linda, and I faced during that time was that my daughter K.C., at 3, did not talk at all and was becoming increasingly difficult to manage. And, when the children came to live with us on Brandywine Street in Philadelphia, Linda not only had a family of four to deal with every day, she had a major-league problem on her hands with K.C.

The neurologist was kind and sensitive, and tried to comfort us, but we were left with a wait-and-see dilemma. We were tortured by a child who seemed constantly in distress, but who could not tell us the cause. My poor child would get on her rocking horse and rock endlessly with a blank look on her face, as if in a trance. There was no manual to tell us what to do. This mystery of life haunted us more than the others.

Was K.C. becoming helplessly autistic and lost in a mental black hole? Or was there something we could do to improve the prospects of her future?

As I think back and remember those bleak moments, I am amazed by Linda's capacity to hang in there and deal with K.C. I really wasn't much help, since I was driven by the demands of my business and did not have much capacity for problems with no logic.

K.C. was almost the age of four as our struggle continued. And then Linda pulled off a miracle of determination.

Linda knew if she could somehow get K.C. to talk, perhaps that would be a beginning to building a more viable personality. But K.C. would only grunt, cry or make gestures when she wanted to indicate some need or displeasure.

One day K.C. was particularly energetic expressing her need for water. Frustrated to the point of exhaustion, and her patience reaching its limit, Linda refused to give K.C. water. Instead she tormented K.C. and challenged her to say "wa wa." K.C. remained stubborn and refused. Linda held her ground and was prepared to let K.C. cry forever.

In time, K.C. grunted what sounded like "wa wa." There it was, however garbled, a breakthrough. K.C. got her water. Linda cried. That precious moment began a new life for K.C.

There would be years of making up for lost ground. Slow at first, K.C. did eventually gain her bearings. She would exceed our wildest expectations, even though her basic disability did not go away.

LIFE GOES ON

Dealing with tragedy and handicaps, and appreciating whatever good fortune came our way, we proceeded forward hopefully.

In 1970 our daughter, Rachel, was born, a beautiful curly redhead who took after Linda's father. Five years later our daughter, Jennifer, was born, a beautiful Italian brunette. That made it four wonderful children: K.C. at 9, Gina 8, Rachel 5, and the new baby.

Our family life was peaceful and full. The kids were growing up. Linda was in perpetual motion dealing with the demands of modern, suburban life: preparing meals, taking care of the house, and driving to and from schools, doctors' offices, stores, and social engagements. Linda was truly the heart of our home, while I allowed my time to be dominated by my business.

We elected not to participate in any religion. Occasionally, we would go to a church or a synagogue for special occasions. This fact saddened my mother, and it sometimes made me wonder if we were making a mistake. I have been hoping it would be enough for our children to adopt the mores of our family life, rather than submitting them to a more formal prescription. Time will tell.

FINANCIAL INDEPENDENCE

Looking back over my 34 years as an independent businessperson, I am proud to say (and it surprises people to hear) that I never experienced a quarter (three-month period) without making a profit. It did not matter if the country was going through a recession or a war, or if technology was turning our world upside down. I would always have my business positioned to get through in a positive manner. There was no room in my psyche for failure and for the resulting embarrassment. If that were to occur, it would likely be for reasons beyond my control.

Occasionally, people ask me to what combination of factors I attribute my exceptional track record.

I feel I began my career in business with an advantage, although it took me a long time before I fully appreciated it. As I mentioned earlier, I was able to view things from both sides of the looking glass. Some people today would call it the ability to think outside the box. Among other things, this capacity prompted me to:

- take my ego out of the equation of business decisions
- employ people smarter and more creative than I am
- know what questions to ask
- understand the business as a whole system, rather than focusing on its various parts without trying to integrate them seamlessly
- realize that the long-term is more important than the short-term
- appreciate that financial independence is worth fighting for
- accept the phenomenon of change as an ever-present factor in the equation of business
- not fight new trends, but try to anticipate them and respond to them as creatively as possible
- ask a lot of questions; move things around, and/or reorganize even when there was no pressing need to

- assume a never-fully-satisfied attitude: If this is good, how do we make it better?
- become strong and as adaptable as possible to prepare the company for both the best of times and the worst of times
- have confidence in my intuition

Blessed with these sensibilities, it did not matter what business I was in. The chances were that I would figure out how to succeed. I started out in the advertising and book publishing businesses, Breig Associates and Dorrance & Company, I sold the latter after starting a graphic arts company. It was from the profits of these businesses that I was able to support Whitmore Publishing Company's excursions into publishing non-subsidized books—42 in all before selling the company. Ultimately, I ended up back in the advertising business (Kingswood Advertising, Inc.).

Over time I withdrew from the management of the day-to-day operations of Kingswood Advertising. I had positioned a very competent person to take over the roles of president and CEO. Rick Moore and I were a good combination. We would be blessed with good fortune for which Rick Moore and the rest of the staff deserve a great deal of the credit.

In my role as chairman, I was the visionary and strategist, free to think and to ask a lot of questions. It was in the later part of 1994 that a really big one began haunting me: "What on earth is the World Wide Web?" The word "Internet" had not yet been uttered by anyone in my company that I knew of. I was beginning to notice it in the press. Something important was on the horizon.

For me, creative inspiration begins with an inquiry. I knew I was asking an important question, although I had yet to express it to anyone. The inspiration that followed was not logical and the odds of it occurring were not very high. Diverse data does not always speak to you and reveal coherent, relevant patterns. I have to review and shuffle the data again and again. Most of the time nothing extraordinary comes from the process.

I will not burden you with details about how I dealt with the opportunities the Internet presented except to say that Kingswood's website won 16 awards in its first year, 1995, and became AOL's site of the day for several weeks. This display of creativity boosted sales along with our status in the advertising community. While we were still seen as the little guy from the standpoint of the much larger agencies in downtown Philadelphia, we were clearly in first place when it came to the World Wide Web. It was an exciting time. By 1997, hardly ten years after establishing Kingswood, it rose within the ranks of agencies in the five-county Philadelphia area from 31st to 9th place. Not only was its sales' curve impressive, its profit picture exceeded our expectation year after year.

The success of our Web initiative more than doubled the value of my company within a year. Should I sell it and cash out? Or should I maintain my controlling interest while enjoying the benefits of ownership in a less active role?

I asked Azza what she thought.

"I am surprised it has taken you so long to get to this point. I think you realize your other aspirations in life can not be achieved while immersed in the affairs of a complex business."

"But, it will be very difficult. After so many years in business I am used to being in charge. A good part of my identity is that of an entrepreneur. Once I walk out that door, I will have lost that."

"You can't fool me, Tony. You never had your heart and soul invested in the business world. To you it was always a means to an end. Others may identify you as a businessman, but that's not how you see yourself. Cash out, Tony. You have been at it long enough. Let others shape the future of Kingswood. Remember the primary goal you established for yourself a long time ago: be free to pursue your other goals without material constraints affecting the outcome. This is a good time to escape, and to use your experience and sensibilities to fulfill the possibilities of The Mazeway Project."

"Thank you, Azza."

My agent, Alan Kalish, found a buyer within a few months. On March 6, 1997, the stockholders of Kingswood Advertising, Inc. sold the assets of the company to John D. Backe, who, earlier in his business career, was President/ CEO of CBS Television. Rick Moore was to remain as President/ CEO of Kingswood. No one would lose his or her job as a result of the sale.

From my point of view, I had hit a home run with the bases loaded in the bottom of the ninth inning in the seventh game of the World Series. I was high for at least two weeks, smiling silently from ear to ear. Of course Linda was also thrilled, since I would no longer be consumed by the endless challenge of being an entrepreneur. I was free.

REFLECTIONS: MY MOTHER AND FATHER

My mother, who is now 96, resides in a Northfield, New Jersey, nursing home. As I write this, she is suffering chronic pain and diminishing memory. And, sad as it is to say, she is failing.

I have always loved her, although it seems not nearly as much earlier in life as I do now. It took more maturity on my part to realize what an extraordinary person she is. I do not know anyone who is as pure and loving, and who practices what she preaches. It is clear that many other people feel the same way. At church she was seen by admirers as a friendly little gray-haired lady struggling to the same front pew each day. That particular pew had been formally dedicated to her and my father many years ago. During the Mass she helped the priest serve Holy Communion. There are special announcements on her birthday, and she receives flowers, gifts, and cards from people she does not know. If there is a heaven, my mother will be there.

My father was more curious and a dreamer. When he discovered there were substantive religions other than Roman Catholicism, he investigated them and tried to understand the differences. One could guess, if he had not married, he would have become a priest or a monk. Teilhard de Chardin, the Jesuit priest who wrote *The Phenomenon of Man* and *The Divine Milieu*, was his hero.

Over the years, he and I discussed religion more than any other subject. My father would almost always find me arguing from a position outside the framework of any formal religion. I was not persuasive enough to lure him through the looking glass to where I stood, and he was unsuccessful at convincing me I should return to his church, but we did respect each other's zeal for seeking truth.

My father died in 1993 at the age of 86. I believe he struggled during his life to reconcile contradictions within himself and within our institutions. I do not know if he made it to the "top of the mountain." I will always love and respect him.

As I look back I feel fortunate to be the product of such good parents and to have enjoyed their loving support.

MY FAMILY TODAY

Our children are now adults scattered about and doing well.

K.C. slowly matured after many years of special education and attention. She became a beautiful, loquacious young lady happily married to Bill Stone. They live in a modest row house in Ardmore, Pennsylvania. K.C. works part-time at a McDonald's restaurant nearby. Bill works at The Merion Cricket Club as a locker-room attendant. They are self-sufficient and live life fully.

Gina holds a Bachelor of Arts in Broadcast Journalism and a Master's Degree in Instructional Design from Ithaca College. She lives in Phoenix, Arizona, with two wonderful children, Caitlin and Blaine, and her partner of four years, Eileen Vincent. Gina has had a long and distinguished career at

Chase Bank, where she is currently an Assistant Vice President of Learning and Development, managing a staff of nine course developers across six sites.

Rachel earned her undergraduate degree from Connecticut College in Anthropology and went on to gain a Master's degree in Acupuncture and Chinese Herbal Medicine from the New England School of Acupuncture. Rachel is married to Paul Budzynski. They live on Nantucket where she practices Acupuncture and Cranial Sacral Therapy. Paul teaches at the Nantucket Lighthouse School. They are the parents of a beautiful baby girl, Isabella.

Jennifer graduated cum laude from Boston University with a major in Psychology and minor in Eastern Religions. Fascinated with the Far East, Jennifer has traveled extensively in Asia, studying different Healing Arts along the way. She then continued her studies and work as a massage therapist in San Francisco for 5 years. There she met her husband, Nicolas Oesch, who is a musician native to Switzerland. They now live outside of Barcelona, Spain, where Jennifer attends a clothing design school.

I am proud of my children. They are strong, sensitive, and independent-minded. I love them very much.

Linda is happy keeping the family connected, managing our social life, and planning the next trip. For me, life in retirement has been good. I am content to spend time reading, dining out, watching movies, traveling, and interacting with friends and family, when I am not working on The Mazeway Project.

Linda and I have traveled a long way together, and have been very fortunate. As I look back, there's no way we could have known how our life would proceed from a remarkable beginning filled with so much sorrow and joy.

NAVIGATING THE MAZEWAY

I *do* realize that, other than the horrific tragedy of Ginny's sudden death, I have lived, and I am living, a charmed life. For this to be the case, I credit, more than anyone else, my parents for their loving support, which allowed me the freedom to navigate the mazeway as I wished. The rest was up to me to work hard and make good choices about family, career, and other aspects of my life.

Did I get to the top of the mountain and gain an inclusive perspective free of contradictions whose premises would be valid forever? Perhaps.

Did I design an educational strategy that would help us, individually and collectively, to become whole and free to fulfill our best possibilities? I do not know at this point. It remains to be seen whether students and others will feel empowered, and are in fact empowered by Life Mapping, Social Mapping, and MetaVisioning. I will be spending a good part of my remaining time and energy to promote these processes.

MY JOURNAL

I started a journal several months after completing my book manuscript. Here are some of the entries.

October 24, 2005

When I watched my mother lie there dying at the end of September, she did not know that my sister, brother, Linda, and I were there. Paralyzed by sorrow, I wondered what regrets about her life she would have mentioned, if she could. I know there were some. I vowed at that moment that I would try as hard as I could for the rest of my own life not to have any unnecessary regrets.

I should mention that the look on my mother's face during the open-casket viewing expressed a beautiful person at peace with herself and the world she left behind. I am sure others were struck by the serenity she exuded, and by how young she looked. During the Catholic Mass commemorating her passing, I presented the following eulogy:

> During the last couple of days, I wondered what I would say about a person I loved unconditionally—a

person who loved me unconditionally—a precious gift gone forever.

Yes, my mother was truly precious. I know many of you agree.

I think it is worth mentioning, for those of you that may not know, that my mother came to this country when she was 11. By the time she was 24, she had three children, and found herself in a desperate situation during the great depression. My father had become ill and was unable to work. The bank foreclosed on our house. My mother tells the story of walking the breadlines in Philadelphia, carrying me in her arms, as my brother, Frank, and my sister, Marie, trailed behind. I can imagine her as a beautiful, young woman, speaking broken English, determined to somehow find a way of getting her family through a horrendous ordeal.

As it turned out, after many years of hard work, my parents became successful in business. Through the decades that followed, they were content to live a simple life, while giving away what they could to children, to grandchildren, to great-grandchildren, to this church, and to other charities. It was in this manner that my mother ended up completing the perfect financial plan. The plan was simple: die penniless.

Of all the smiles I ever saw on my mother's face, the biggest of them all was when she learned that every bit of the expense of her stay at the Meadowview Nursing Home would be *free*. It would be free because she qualified for Medicaid. It thrilled her to know that she would *not* be a burden on her children.

Yes, my mother was truly precious. I will always love her.

November 12, 2005

I am pleased to say that Resources for Human Development (www.rhd.org) has become the coordinating sponsor of The

Mazeway Project. RHD is a diverse, not-for-profit corporation established in 1970. It employs over 3,000 persons and currently directs over 140 human service programs in 11 states and the District of Columbia. Its central office is located in Philadelphia, Pennsylvania.

RHD programs serve over 12,000 people each year through outreach, day treatment, outpatient treatment, youth, educational, and residential services. It fosters ideas and programs that are innovative, effective, caring, and efficient. The corporation embraces the value that all human beings are of equal worth, and it is committed to providing a service atmosphere of empowerment, trust, and respect.

I am proud to say that I have been a member of RHD's Board of Directors for over 30 years, and have watched its range of programs expand dramatically, and its budget grow from $1 million to $125 million.

While it is expected that other institutions will be involved in The Mazeway Project, RHD will function as its coordinating sponsor. Its grant-writing staff will be developing proposals to help raise funds for orchestrating the various programs of the project: (1) its website; (2) programs involving educational institutions; (3) online Life Mapping and Social Mapping courses; (4) MetaVisioning; (5) Mazeway Forums; and (6) Mazeway Networking.

November 19, 2005

I have the good fortune to know Dr. Ashok Gangadean, a Professor of Philosphy at Haverford College. Professor Gangadean is involved in many initiatives beyond the campus, such as: the Global Dialogue Institute, Logos Institute, World Wisdom Council, The World Commission of Global Consciousness & Spirituality, and the Greater Philadelphia Philosophy Consortium. I was amazed by what I found when I checked out these organizations on the Internet. Some of those involved in these initiatives are among the most gifted and respected people walking the planet.

Professor Gangadean invited me to send him a summary of The Mazeway Project. He responded: "I see lots of deep links with my own work and outlook." This led to a meeting with him, during which it became clear that his aspirations and mine regarding humankind's developmental journey have a lot in common. While I do not function at the same level of sophistication as Professor Gangadean, I appreciate his vision of the need for humankind to transcend our egocentric worldview, so that we may awaken our global mind and help give birth to higher forms of global cultures and worlds.

Given how complementary our perspectives and goals are, we agreed to meet again and work together to relate The Mazeway Project to some of his own initiatives, especially the Global Dialogue Institute of which he is a co-founder. He appointed me an Associate of the Institute.

December 9, 2005

I wonder whether an appeal for support will convince board members of one foundation or another that our system of education remains extraordinarily fragmented, inefficient, self-limiting, and somewhat out of control—that the problem is not so much the lack of money as it is systemic and conceptual. How will we find the words to describe succinctly the processes of Life Mapping, Social Mapping, and MetaVisioning, and how they would introduce strategic variables into the equation of the educational process that, in the fullness of time, would help transform the system from the inside out?

I also wonder if I will be able to convince any colleges that they have much to gain and little to lose by offering experimental courses in Life Mapping, Social Mapping, and MetaVisioning. Will they be impressed that we have the support of Resources for Human Development and the possibility of a grant from a foundation? Can they imagine that, if the students affirm the The Mazeway Project by way of their enthusiastic reaction, grants and other support may flow into the institution, as a vision concerning how to refresh K-16 curricula reveals itself?

January 1, 2006

"Happy New Year, Azza!"

"Happy New Year, Tony. I must say that it seems that a lot of things are now falling into place for you, Tony, regarding The Mazeway Project. Your perseverance and hard work are paying off. You are managing to offset the disadvantage of 'being nobody from nowhere,' as you characterize yourself. Actually, you may be close to generating a very uncommon synergy by combining your book, a website, the support of RHD, the support of a foundation, and the involvement of colleges. Assembling this combination is very important since your book alone will not be sufficient to propel the project forward."

"Azza, I am wondering what you think of the idea of involving someone with more credentials and more evolved than I am to direct The Mazeway Project. As you will recall, that's what I did so often during my business career. I was better at envisioning what we should do next than I was doing the work necessary to fulfill the vision."

"I understand what you are saying, Tony. However, this is not like anything you have envisioned in business. At least, initially, this project may require your direct participation along with your unique passion and your energy. I wonder why you underrate your capacity as a social entrepreneur."

"It's not a matter of being modest and underestimating my capacity. The Mazeway Project will require many more years of hard work to fulfill its possibilities. Consequently, my age will become a factor. Therefore, it will be wise to have someone involved who could continue on. And then there is the reality that the project may be so far-reaching that it requires a modern-day Renaissance person to lead it forward, rather than someone with my limitations."

"Yes, Tony. I understand. Perhaps you will find that special person after the book is published and some of the other pieces of the puzzle fall into place."

March 17, 2006

As I grow older, I wonder if my book and my Life Map will represent my "message in a bottle" for those who follow. I do not believe it will be the material things that I leave behind.

I think I understand why children don't ask elders very often what they think and feel. They get tired of the preaching, as I had gotten tired of it as a youngster. This is why I don't say very much to my children regarding how they should live their life. Just as I wanted to be free to model my life based on my own sensibilities, they should be free to decide what's best for them. I think my children know I will always be there to help them, if they need me.

May 25, 2006

I wonder what would happen if all those who seek elective office had to assemble their Life Map and Social Map, and present them to the public. Since all the candidates would be using the same mapping templates, this would enable voters to perceive and compare the candidates in a comprehensive and systematic manner. Furthermore, the performance of those elected could be tracked relative to what they articulated in their maps. I think we would be amazed by what our communities and nation would gain from this simple strategy.

October 11, 2006

Clearly, The Mazeway Project is already gaining momentum.

At Muhlenberg College the process of Life Mapping was introduced this term to 75 freshmen within a course on Wellness taught by Professor Linda Andrews. I will soon be receiving copies of Life Maps that the students assembled. I was invited to attend two of the classes during which the students asked me questions. In turn, I had the opportunity to ask them questions. I was fascinated by the experience and amazed how gracefully Professor Andrews had guided students through the process of Life Mapping.

At Drexel University the reception I have received has been extraordinary. I had sent a letter to Dr. Constantine Papadakis, the President of Drexel, along with a seven-page summary of The Mazeway Project. In my letter I said: "Because the integration of knowledge is one of its primary objectives, the initiative does not fit easily within any one discipline. Therefore, I would appreciate your help to delineate who among your faculty could direct such a project. I imagine it would be someone who might be called a modern-day Renaissance person, rather than someone who is an expert in one discipline or another, and not interested in the challenge of helping students 'connect the dots' and comprehend things holistically. I would appreciate it if you would let me know to whom I should talk about this possibility."

The document and letter were forwarded to the College of Arts and Sciences and ended up in the hands of Professor Douglas V. Porpora, who heads the Department of Culture and Communications. I was invited to lunch with him and the Director of Development of the college, Bela R. Banker. After three meetings during this past summer and after reading my manuscript, Dr. Porpora invited me to teach a course at Drexel next spring on the subjects of Life Mapping and Social Mapping. I was very surprised to say the least. I was also surprised by the reception I received from the Dean of the College of Arts and Sciences, Donna Murasko. She was aware of the meetings I had with Professor Porpora and Mrs. Banker, and seemed impressed with what she knew about The Mazeway Project. She and Professor Porpora suggested that I work with professors from six different disciplines within her college to evaluate their reactions to the processes of Life Mapping and Social Mapping. Also, it was proposed that I have the assistance of a graduate student to further refine my work and to help prepare me to teach the course next spring.

A couple of weeks later, I was invited to meet with Dean Murasko again. It was then that she invited me to become a member of her Advisory Board.

October 27, 2006

To help promote my book, it was suggested that Professor Porpora write a "blurb" that could be used on the back cover of my book. He readily accepted, and, within a few days, I had the first formal review of my work. This prompted me to ask two other educators to review my manuscript: Dr. Howard Clark Kee and Dr. Judith S Miller. Here is what the three of them wrote, starting with Dr. Porpora:

> Our educational system—colleges included—is letting us down. So argues Anthony J. Parrotto in *Navigating the Mazeway*. We are not being taught to ask the big, synthesizing questions that "put it all together." We are not being taught to question the assumptions underlying our world views, the life assumptions we have written on our own "page zero." Instead, our education socializes us into specialization and fragmentation.
>
> *Navigating the Mazeway* is a remarkable call for us to move beyond narrow, technical reason and to think more broadly about the directions in which we are collectively moving. The book is written in plain language accessible to all. Most important, Parrotto's templates for "life mapping" and "social mapping" provide valuable tools for us to reason together on the major issues of life. The book and the templates are an especially promising way to get students to integrate their educational experience.
>
> Douglas Porpora, Ph. D.
> Chairperson: Department of Culture & Communications, College of Arts and Sciences, Drexel University. Author of *Landscapes of the Soul: The Loss of Moral Meaning in American Life*

Navigating the Mazeway is a remarkable book that makes us aware of how our educational institutions have led us astray, and that our only hope in the 21st century lies in the journey back to ourselves. What causes this book to stand out among the rest is that the author gently and creatively guides readers through the "Mazeway" so that they actually discover their deepest and most authentic selves. With erudite scholarship, down-to-earth practicality, psychological sophistication, and the "mind of God," Mr. Parrotto guides seekers through the Mazeway so that they may reach their potential as human beings. In so doing, he clearly convinces us that taking this journey is not only a personal gift of empowerment, but also a necessity for our culture and global humanity at this time in evolution. Parrotto accomplishes in this ingenious book what our educational and societal institutions have not been able to. A visionary masterpiece that may be just what our civilization has been looking for.
Judith S. Miller Ph.D.
Adj. Professor of Human Development, Teachers College, Columbia University. Author of *Direct Connection: Transformation of Consciousness*

I found *Navigating the Mazeway* to be deeply perceptive and informative in a wide range of academic fields. The basic theme concerns human life, individually and socially, and the call is for the reader to gain fuller and deeper understanding of one's self, and to perceive how one can gain and maintain meaning, purpose, and fulfillment in life in constructive and helpful service to others.

The proposal is for one to engage in careful and comprehensive analysis of one's life, the influence of family, social context, education and life experience. The author has developed a dual method to enable one to achieve these objectives: one focus is on social setting and influences; the other is on one's personal experience of helps and difficulties. Rather than merely articulate the theoretical objectives, Mr. Parrotto has advanced specific and detailed methods by which this self-analysis can be developed.

In Chapter Two he points out to the reader the wide range of factors which shape life and which, when examined carefully in our experience, provide insights and influences which affect our life. The reader is urged to see how these elements have influenced one's life and thinking, personal and social relationships, and how they shape one's values–economic and moral–as well as one's perspective on the future.

In this undertaking the author has drawn upon an impressive range of intellectual, academic disciplines: historical, philosophical, psychological and sociological. Of particular importance for the book as a whole is the call to the reader to examine critically and to perceive fruitfully the nature, sources and range of one's knowledge. The Life Map that the reader is urged to develop focuses on one's individual, personal experience; the Social Map calls the reader to become aware of the range of social influences which were major factors in developing one's perception of personal identity, life goals, social and moral values.

To achieve and articulate these impressive insights, the author has employed methods and insights especially from the philosophical feature called epistemology–the theoretical ground of human knowledge–and from sociology: the analysis of group identity and values. This book has the potential to contribute to students and scholars fresh and deeper understanding in the natural and social sciences, in art, literature, history, medicine and law. It provides insights for personal and group identity, and for perceiving the aims and values in one's career.

Howard Clark Kee, Ph. D.
Professor of Religion Emeritus of Graduate Studies and Religion at Boston University, and Visiting Scholar at University of Pennsylvania. He is the author of several acclaimed books, including *Understanding the New Testament* and *The Cambridge Companion to the Bible*.

My reaction to these reviews: tears.

January 1, 2007

2006 was a good year for The Mazeway Project and for me personally. I was pleased how well the various elements of my book manuscript came together to form a clear overview of what I think and feel about humankind's predicament, and what we can do about it. Given my limitations, I thought the chances were high that I would make some serious mistakes that might discredit the rest of what I had to say. This did not occur. Instead, I received affirmation from a diverse range of individuals who convinced me that my premises are valid and that The Mazeway Project should be taken seriously. My interactions with professors at Haverford, Bryn Mawr, and Muhlenberg colleges, together with interactions with professors at Drexel, Pennsylvania, and Columbia Universities provided encouraging feedback. The invitation from Drexel to teach a course on Life Mapping and Social Mapping surprised me. Also surprising were the pre-publication reviews of my book and the fact that I was readily able to assemble an Advisory Board for The Mazeway Project comprising highly evolved individuals from a diverse range of prestigious institutions.

Please Note

After this book goes to press, I will be posting additional entries to My Journal on the website. And, if there is another edition of this book, I will add the new journal entries.

If you wish to comment on any aspect of what I have written, please email me at tparrotto@rhd.org.

GLOSSARY

Asymptotic Refers to a process by which something is always getting closer to something else but never reaches it. Seeking truth is considered by some to be an asymptotic process.

Body Wisdom We, as individuals, normally know more about many of the subtleties and peculiarities of our own bodies than physicians or instruments can discern. The more knowledge we accrue about how to manage our bodies and maintain full health, the better—and the greater likelihood of realizing our life expectancy.

Bureaucracy An administrative system characterized by standardized procedures, formal division of responsibility, hierarchy, and impersonal relationships. Typically, such systems operate without utilizing feedback and self-correction. As a result, they may become highly inefficient, inflexible, and uncreative.

Coherence The quality of being logically or aesthetically consistent, with all separate parts fitting together to form a harmonious and credible whole. Within the context of Life Mapping and Social Mapping, the challenge is to reconcile variables in a manner that is free of contradictions.

Conceptual Imprisonment Through social conditioning, fear, a lack of curiosity, and a highly fragmented educational process, most of us are imprisoned conceptually within a twilight zone of awareness in which we delude ourselves that we are oriented and free in the mazeway.

Egocentric Perspective An exclusive orientation that precludes the capacity to identify with other perspectives. Within an egocentric perspective, we do not question our premises; we simply seek affirmation of what we already believe, while ignoring the possibility of adopting a more inclusive and more empowering perspective.

Emotional Wisdom Awareness of our feelings and the feelings of others that enables us to direct our lives sensitively and creatively.

Entropy A measure of the disorder that exists in a system.

Fragmented Curriculum An array of subjects covered in an educational program within which the subjects remain largely disconnected from one another, making it difficult, if not impossible, for students to form an integrated perception of themselves and the world around them.

Generalists Function at a higher level of integration than most Specialists can achieve. Either by training or by natural inclination they are able to discern the connections among a wider range of disparate elements of knowledge and of organizational structure. Their unique attribute gives them the capacity to capture a sense of the big picture—to see things more holistically. They know intuitively the strategic questions that should be asked, while having the wherewithal otherwise to orchestrate a complex array of political and operational variables.

Illusion A false idea, conception, or belief. Something that deceives the senses or mind by appearing to exist when it does not, or appearing to be one thing when it is in fact another.

Integral Worldview A perspective that honors the truths of each outlook that has come before, while proceeding forward to compose a coherent, integrated perspective.

Learning Organization A learning organization has the capacity to enhance its capabilities and shape its own future. It constitutes any organization (e.g., school, business, government agency) that understands itself as a complex, organic system that uses feedback systems and alignment mechanisms to achieve its goals. Within a learning organization people continually expand their capacity to create the results they truly desire, where new and expansive patterns of thinking are nurtured, where collective aspiration is set free, and where people are continually learning to see the whole together.[47]

Life Mapping The conscious process of developing a comprehensive Life Map that leads to an overall sense of who we are and how we may orchestrate an authentic, satisfying life.

Life Map Template A matrix constituting 16 elements that structure the process of Life Mapping.

Malleable General Masses We are part of the malleable general masses within the social process, when our minds and hearts can be shaped and perhaps reshaped by the programs of the mind espoused by institutions and individuals.

Mazeway The mazeway constitutes you, me, and everyone else, functioning within the social process of this planet, situated in the riddle of the universe—a puzzle within a puzzle within a puzzle.

MetaVisionaries We may call them prophets, shamans, and mystics. As extraordinary as they are rare, these individuals are positioned at the very top of the hierarchy of humankind's mental and spiritual capacities. MetaVisionaries not only possess the attributes of Visionaries; they are also able to access the mind of God *within* them as well as the mind of God *beyond* them, as if there were no distinction. At least that is how it may be perceived by the MetaVisionary and/or by his or her interpreters and, in turn, by those who follow. While all of us may possess godlike attributes, MetaVisionaries have the capacity to function *like God* per se, if only as an intermediary. It's as though they reached *the* top of the mountain and were able to perceive an endless horizon and beyond in a seamless, integral manner, and to feel an inherent part of it all, if only fleetingly.

MetaVisioning Instead of waiting for a MetaVisionary to come along to guide us through and beyond the turmoil of modern times, we can choose to work together to generate a MetaVision ourselves. We may refer to this as a Social Map of Social Maps—a coherent, overarching vision of how we can move forward together creatively, joyfully, and peacefully as a species. One way of doing this is through open-source collaboration—a special kind of online interaction that amplifies our *combined* wisdom.

Mind of God Within May be defined as a gestalt of our mental faculties—the sum of our thoughts, feelings, intuition, imagination, and conscience. The combination of these attributes, functioning in an integrated, resonant manner, can propel us to a higher level of consciousness within which we transcend the limits of our sensory faculties. In this special state, we experience a direct connection to the infinite-enfolded truth of quantum reality—clarity of knowing beyond knowledge—a sense of time before time—a glimpse of the whole, seamless vision of the mazeway. As an inherent part of the implicate order, the mind of God within us is the ultimate moral compass, the source of creativity, the means to our liberation and further development.

Modern Worldview The modern worldview emerged when travel increased and exposure to other cultures took place. An ever increasing number of people recognized that there were realities different from their own. This insight prompted some individuals and groups to propose new ideas that were at odds with the established order of things, i.e., premodern worldview.

Myth A traditional story about heroes or supernatural beings that tries to explain the origins of natural phenomena or aspects of human behavior. Fictitious or not, a myth can become the premise of the program of the mind that empowers a major institution.

Our True Self We have two identities. One is imposed by the culture around us; the other comprises our true self—the essence of our uniqueness at the core of our being which would express itself if we were free and empowered. Most of us are conceptually imprisoned and will never realize our true identity. This is because the programs of the mind advanced by our institutions are so commanding that it is very difficult for us to transcend them.

Page Zero Premises These are basic premises that underpin programs of the mind. At the core of each program, on its Page Zero, is a set of premises which empowers the program.

Postmodern Worldview The perception of sociologists, psychologists, and others that programs of the mind are social constructions of reality. This means that all ideas about human reality are social inventions created by human beings—that what is "real" and what is "not real" are not determined by an external deity, but by the way we see, name and classify our experience through language. Therefore, since the programs of the mind were conceived and developed by humans, we are free to modify or reinvent them for our time. Instead of *absolute* values ordained by a deity *or* generated through human inquiry, there are only *relative* values based on the context of the situation.

Premodern Worldview Premodern worldviews were based *either* on a claimed revelation *or* on human inquiry. A "revealed" worldview constituted a perception of reality that emerged gradually, took hold and, typically, became a fixed belief system *perceived to be engendered by a god* and sustained by tradition. Examples of revealed worldviews are to be found in Judaism, Christianity, and Islam. On the other hand, a "non-revealed" worldview constituted a perception of reality that also emerged gradually, took hold, and was sustained by tradition. But, instead of being ordained by a god, *it was generated through human inquiry*, that is, through the thoughts, feelings, and imagination of individuals. Examples of non-revealed worldviews include Buddhism and Taoism.

Programs of Mind Constitute thought patterns we acquire through exposure to our culture. Religion, government, schools and the family are the institutions primarily responsible for "installing" programs of the mind. These include traditions, ideologies, theories, and other social constructs promulgated by our institutions for understanding how the world works and how we fit into it. Most of us follow programs of the mind without understanding their premises or exploring their rationale. Programs of the mind teach us to be faithful and stay within bounds, as if inoculated against other points of view.

Quantum Reality A reality which exists outside of our time and space, and is linked to it through our consciousness. Quantum Reality has within it infinite, enfolded truth (the implicate order), which, through our consciousness and in other ways, affects the reality of our own time and space (the explicate order).

Relativism Those who are relativists believe that the meaning and value of human beliefs and behaviors have no absolute reference. They claim that humans understand and evaluate beliefs and behaviors only in terms of the context of the situation.

Self-catalyzing, self-cleansing, sustainable institution Designed to function *organically* with checks, balances, and internal feedback loops that help catalyze and cleanse the system in a manner that spawns creativity, sustainability, and further development. Currently, most institutions function *bureaucratically*, with a traditional top-down organizational construct that lacks these attributes.

Selfless Refers to a mental state in which personal security and happiness are seen as secondary to a higher purpose. We become selfless by taking our identity from our soul rather than our ego–when we pursue creativity as an end in itself.

Social Mapping The process of working closely and patiently with others to build vibrant and sustainable institutions and communities that reflect the heightened awareness of ourselves and of the great issues of our time.

Social Process The dynamic interplay among political, economic, and cultural institutions.

Socio-Economic Machine The elaborate set of hierarchies by which almost all our institutions are organized. Top-down bureaucratic methods of structuring can be found everywhere: in government, business, religion, and education. When the entire set of hierarchies is put together, it forms the socio-economic machine. Each part of the machine—each hierarchy, each particular institution—is dedicated to maintaining its structure and perpetuating its functions. Whether it be a political, economic or cultural institution, it uses its power to stay in existence—to maintain the status quo or gain more power and control.

Specialists Include scientists, physicians, lawyers, jurists, accountants, teachers, scholars, economists, politicians, priests, ministers, and rabbis, along with experts in other fields. Specialists can be highly useful to us because their orientation embodies knowledge and skills that may help us deal with one aspect or another of our lives.

Spiritual Wisdom We accrue spiritual wisdom when we are quiet and peaceful, and motivated by love and selflessness. Only then can we resonate with the coherent patterns of the mazeway and gain a coherent, inclusive perspective.

Transcendence In religion, transcendence is a condition or mode of being that is independent of physical existence.

Truth-Seeking Machine The process of distilling truth through deep dialogue among those of us who are dedicated to systematically mapping our own lives, and to exploring beyond ourselves in an effort to generate coherent Social Maps that help us actualize our best possibilities as a society.

Twilight Zone of Health When someone is neither in full health nor in a state of disease, he or she is in a subtle state of health between the two.

Universal Worldview An inclusive perspective free of contradictions, whose premises would be valid forever.

Values Each of us has a core of underlying values that contribute to our system of beliefs, ideas, and/or opinions. Our values form the basis from which we operate or react. They may or may not be entirely in agreement with the prevailing values of the culture within which we find ourselves.

Visionaries These are highly gifted individuals who evolve to a very high level of awareness. By their nature, and perhaps somewhat by training, they have a much greater sense of how the *larger chunks* of the big picture fit together. Somehow, as established paradigms become exhausted of their energy, visionaries are able to discern coherent patterns within what appears to others to be mostly chaos. Or they may simply perceive an even better way of doing something that is still working satisfactorily.

BOOKSHELF & REFERENCES

1. Anderson, W.T. *Reality Isn't What It Used to Be.* Harper San Francisco, 1990.
2. Beck, Don Edward and Cowan, Christopher C. *Spiral Dynamics.* Blackwell Publishers, 1996.
3. Birch, Charles, and Cobb, John B. Jr. *The Liberation of Life*. Cambridge: Cambridge University Press, 1981.
4. Brenden, Barbara. *The Passion of Ayn Rand*. Doubleday & Company, 1986
5. Bohm, David. *Wholeness and the Implicate Order*. London: Ark Paperbacks, 1983.
6. Bronowski, J. *The Ascent of Man*. Little Brown and Co., 1973.
7. Capra, Fritjof. *The Turning Point*. Bantam Books, 1983.
8. Clark, Kenneth. *Civilization*. New York: Harper and Row. 1969.
9. d'Aquili, Eugene G. and Newberg, Andrew B. *The Mystical Mind*. Fortress Press, 1999.
10. Elias, John L. *Conscientization and Deschooling.* The Westminster Press, 1976
11. Dubos, Rene. *So Human an Animal*. Charles Scribner's Sons, 1968.
12. Durant, Will. *The Story of Civilization*. Simon and Schuster, 1954.
13. Fadiman, Clifton, and Major, John S. *The New Lifetime Reading Plan*. Harper Perennial, 1998.
14. Frankl, Viktor E. *Man's Search for Meaning*. Washington Square Press, 1969.
15. Friedman, Thomas. L. *The World Is Flat*. Farrar, Straus and Giroux, 2005.
16. Fromm, Erich. *To Have or To Be?* Harper & Row, 1976.
17. Fromm, Erich. *The Heart of Man*. Harper & Row, 1964.
18. Fuller, Buckminster. *Operating Manual for Spaceship Earth*.
19. Gangadean, Ashok K. *Between Worlds: The Emergence of Global Reason*. Peter Lang, 1998.
20. Garcia, John David. *Creative Transformation*. Whitmore Publishing Co., 1991.
21. Garcia, John David. *Psychofraud and Ethical Therapy*. Whitmore Publishing Co., 1974.
22. Garcia, John David. *The Moral Society*. The Julian Press, Inc., 1973.
23. Halle, Louis J. *Out of Chaos*. Houghton Mifflin, 1977.
24. Hawking, Stephen. *A Brief History of Time*. Bantam, 1988.
25. Hirsch, E.D. *The Schools We Need and Why We Don't Have Them*. Doubleday, 1996.
26. Hoyle, Fred. *The Intelligent Universe*. Holt, Reinhart and Winston, 1983.

27. Illich, Ivan. *Deschooling Society*. Harper & Row, 1971.
28. C.C. Jung. *The Undiscovered Self*. The New American Library, 1957.
29. Kee, Howard Clark. *Knowing the Truth: A Sociological Approach to New Testament Interpretation.* Fortress Press, 1987.
30. Kvale, Steinar. *Themes of Postmodernity. (The Truth About The Truth).* Putnam, 1995.
31. Ervin Laszlo. *The Connectivity Hypothesis*. State University of New York Press, 2003.
32. McLaughlin, Corinne, and Davidson, Gordon. *Spiral Politics*. Ballantine Books, 1994.
33. Maslow, A.H. *The Further Reaches of Human Nature*. The Viking Press, 1973.
34. Maslow, A.H. *Toward a Psychology of Being.* Van Nostrand Reinhold, 1968.
35. Mellert, Robert B. *What Is Process Theology?* Paulist Press, 1975.
36. Miller, Judith S. *Direct Connection*. Rutledge Books, 2000.
37. Myss, Caroline. *Anatomy of the Spirit*. Three Rivers Press, 1996.
38. Parrotto, Anthony. *Baldness, Grayness: Treatable or Non-Treatable?* Whitmore Publishing Co., 1961.
39. Platt, John R. *The Step to Man*. John Wiley and Sons, 1966.
40. Pirsig, Robert M. *Zen and the Art of Motorcycle Maintenance*. Bantam Books, 1974.
41. Porpora, Douglas. *Landscapes of the Soul.*
42. Prigogine, Ilya and Stengers, Isabelle. *Order Out of Chaos.* Bantam Books, 1984.
43. Rand, Ayn. *The Voice of Reason; Essays in Objectivist Thought.* Meridian Books, 1989.
44. Reimer, Everett. *School Is Dead: Alternatives in Educa*tion. Doubleday, 1971.
45. Restivo, Sal. *The Sociological Worldview*. Basil Blackwell, 1991.
46. Salk, Jonas. *The Survival of the Wisest*. Harper & Row, 1973.
47. Senge, Peter. *The Fifth Discipline: The Art and Practice of the Learning Organization*. Random House, 1990.
48. Skinner, B.F. *Beyond Freedom and Dignity.* Bantam Books, 1971.
49. Teilhard de Chardin, Pierre. *The Phenomenon of Man*. Harper & Row, 1965.
50. Teilhard de Chardin, Pierre. *The Heart of Matter*. Harcourt Brace Jovanovich, 1976.
51. Toffler, Alvin. *The Third Wave*. William Morrow, 1980.
52. Tyndall, Dr. Ann. *Body Wisdom. Healthy, Wealthy & Wise*, 1996.

53. Walsh, Roger, and Vaughan, Frances. *Paths Beyond Ego.* Jeremy P. Tarcher / Perigee Books, 1993.
54. Whitehead, Alfred North. *Adventures of Ideas*. The Macmillan Company, 1933.
55. Wikipedia.org
56. Wilber, Ken. *A Brief History of Everything*. Shambhala Publications, 1996.
57. Wilber, Ken. *Quantum Questions.* Shambhala Publications, 1984.